ENDORSEMENTS

"With great vulnerability, Jeanie exposes the frailty of her journey through brokenness and trauma. You will be deeply encouraged by her pursuit of wholeness and her passionate devotion to Christ."

Cynthia Spell,

M.A., M.S.

Biblical Counselor in Private Practice

Cynthialspell@gmail.com

"I can still recall one of my earlier meetings with Jeanie. She had made an appointment to see me at my office. and when she arrived, she carried a guitar and after greeting me, commenced to singing an original song she felt the Lord had given her for me. Needless to say, it made quite an impression.

Mike and Jeanie were members of our small church in Florida for many years, and I was able to hear several more songs over that time shared as an encouragement for myself or our church. One thing we could be sure of, she was never boring or unoriginal. I believe every church needs someone to provide that little extra seasoning, as she did.

In her book, Jeanie provides a brutally honest look into her life as a follower of Jesus, and addresses issues the church has often been reticent to tackle. Mental and spiritual wellness are the business of the church, yet we often find the mental part uncomfortable.

Jeanie's unique voice guides us through her own journey through humor and poetry and above all, a brave self-revelation of her struggles as well as God's providential guidance that has carried her through life.

I would recommend this book to anyone who struggles with inner storms, whose searching for peace and needing a friendly voice to accompany them on that expedition."

Rob Woodrum, Pastor of Eastgate Christian Fellowship,
Panama City Beach, Florida

"I met Jeanie in 2006 at a women's conference in Panama City, Florida. While getting a cup of coffee, she came up behind me and said, 'God told me we were going to be friends.' I didn't know it yet, but when Jeanie said God told her something, she wasn't kidding.

Over the years I have come to know her as a faithful friend and a fearsome prayer warrior. She is one of the few people I can call at any time for prayer, counsel, or encouragement.

Her testimony could be construed as a failure of medicine and current psychiatric therapy, but that would be missing the point completely. Her story is one of God's faithfulness and the triumph that comes through Him.

This book will be an inspiration to anyone who has ever struggled with mental illness or the discouragement that comes from trying and failing to be a better or different person.

Jeanie's love for God and people, and the joy with which she lives her life come through clearly. I hope you enjoy this book as much as I have enjoyed her friendship."

Kymberly Rittman, D.O. ACOFP

"Jeanie is a minstrel minister, and her song lyrics and engaging life-story drew me in. Before you know it, you are entering her journey, relating to portions that perhaps have been experienced by you, and then finding the healing that she received! With raw and vulnerable truth delineating the pain she endured, Jeanie is also just as raw and vulnerable about what only Jesus can do—He who often works through process and doctors and our continual surrender to Him. What an example she is to show the way for healing that is true! I have known Jeanie for two decades. She is the real deal, and her realness is a gift you need to unwrap!"

Pastor Paul W. Kummer

Former pastor of Grace Lutheran Church, Destin, Florida

Presently serving on pastoral staff at Bethel Church,

Redding, Callifornia

"I met Jeanie and Michael shortly after they moved to Franklin in 2019.

As an author and founder of Simple Truths and Successories, Inc., I agreed to read her manuscript. I discovered transparency and vulnerability as she shares her journey to sound mental health. As her chapters take you on a roller coaster, I encourage you to hold on till the end. It's worth the ride!"

Mac Anderson, author of twenty-two books
that sold more than three million copies,
including *Change is Good…You Go First;*
212°: The Extra Degree; **The Dash***;*
To a Child, Love Is Spelled T-I-M-E;
and *What's the Big Idea?*

PROMISE
YOU WON'T
REMEMBER

BECOMING WHOLE WHEN
PIECES ARE MISSING

JEANIE M. CONNELL

Selah Press

PUBLISHING
NASHVILLE, TENNESSEE

DEDICATION

Romans 10:9 says:
"If you declare with your mouth
that Jesus is Lord
and believe in your heart
that God raised Him from the dead,
you will be saved."

Delivered. Rescued. His child.

Dedicated to Abba Father, who gave
the assignment to write my God story.
He's the One who knows me best
And loves me most.

CONTENTS

FOREWORD

My wife Meg and I first met Jeanie at Aqueduct Conference Center when I was teaching from my latest book, *Defeating Dark Angels*. During the weekend, we recognized her gift of thinking in song. She put melodies and lyrics to people, God's Word, and life taking place around her. Before we parted, my wife and I, along with five others, gathered in the prayer chapel for a prayer session with Jeanie. The transformation we witnessed before we said our goodbyes was amazing! 2 Corinthians 3:17 (NIV) says, "Now the Lord is Spirit, and where the Lord is, there is freedom."

Jeanie, when I met her, was a forty-year-old woman, married, and mother of three children. She seemed to be a happy, committed Christian, and she was very active in ministering to others. However, she had been badly abused sexually and in other ways as a youngster. After ten years of professional therapy, she was still carrying a considerable load of hurt inside. In our prayer session, we walked with Jesus through each hurtful event. Jesus took the load and set her free.

Jeanie later wrote me that the freedom she experienced that day was the most life-changing thing that's ever happened to her.

This book is the story of God at work in Jeanie's life. You will see how freedom leads to intimacy with God. She beautifully describes her struggles and how she dealt with them in her daily walking with God. You will clearly see how she has been healed of her "condition" that she'd lived with her whole life. She has now found peace and freedom inside. May you join Jeanie and let the Holy Spirit guide you to greater freedom and intimacy with God.

Charles H. Kraft
Retired Professor, Fuller Theological Seminary.
In healing ministry for more than 30 years

PREFACE

I want to tell you a little about how this book came about.

In Spencer, North Carolina, in 1994, God spoke to me about the dark tunnel I was walking through, assuring me I would reach the light. When? I didn't know. He wanted me to write a book called, *I Wasn't Sexually Abused, So Why am I Hurting?*

With our youngest child entering kindergarten, I wrote a 250-page manuscript and retired it to our bookshelf.

After I moved to Panama City Beach, Florida, in 2003, I began rewriting my story with a new title, *Consider It Pure Joy*, taken from James 1:2–4. I was invited to share my testimony at church with a group of women, who each had memories of personal child sexual abuse. As I prepared to speak to them rewriting my story, I thought I would have more memories. I didn't. I put the second draft back on the shelf. Even after ten years of psychotherapy, I still had no memories. Before age ten it seemed, I did not exist.

What I did remember was Mom's mantra: "Promise you won't remember!"

I had my own mantra: Deuteronomy 29:29, which says:

"The secret things belong to the Lord our God, but the things revealed belong to us and to our children forever, that we may do all the words of this law."

I wrote my story a third time because I knew there were others who believed they could be whole if they could recover their past. I wrote because I knew there were others who searched for answers to misplaced anger, addictions, and deleted memories.

I have a co-author named C.J., which stands for Child Jeanie. I did not believe she existed until 1983 when I began counseling. Aside from ten human professionals, I needed C.J. to help me grow up.

God speaks to me in a quiet, loving voice that others can't hear. He also speaks to me in songs that I can share with others. My chapters end with those songs. They are my memories.

INTRODUCTION

My story intersects with yours if you or anyone you know has become addicted. An addiction doesn't have to be drugs or alcohol or sex—mine wasn't. One important thing I know is that no one sets out to develop an addiction. I certainly didn't. No one does.

My story intersects with yours if you lived without memories from certain times in your life and wondered why or how to retrieve them.

My story intersects with yours if you have grown up believing your family was healthy and well-adjusted, only to find out otherwise as an adult.

I had a father who provided for his family, who attended church, and loved God. I longed for a father who called me princess, or precious, or his little one. The roots of that longing went deep—deep inside my heart, soul, and mind. It was my secret. If anyone knew my secret, they would think I was selfish and ungrateful because I was fortunate to have my dad.

I learned that having a diagnosis is not a bad thing. It's something that helps us understand how God made us, how we function, and how to love ourselves rather than compare ourselves to others. I will share my diagnosis inside these pages.

I will take you behind the closed door of professional counseling sessions—ten years of psychotherapy, counseling, and two psychiatric hospitals, in search of memories. Most chapters end with an original song that put melody and lyrics to my life.

I'm hoping in writing this memoir, it will encourage others who have had similar struggles and assist professional counselors who are trying to help patients like me.

May you reach the light at the end of your tunnel,

Jeanie Connell

Chapter 1
THE FAST

The day before my forty-third birthday, Sunday, December 27, 1992, our pastor at Foursquare church in Salisbury, North Carolina, challenged his small congregation to a fast. I knew fasting went hand in hand with prayer, but to me, this fast represented life and death.

I don't fast. I hadn't fasted except from sweets or soft drinks during Lent. I didn't know anyone else who fasted, but on that day, we were asked to choose something in our life that we placed great importance on. Anything we felt we couldn't live without—and not necessarily food. Something that had become more important than our relationship with Jesus.

Immediately, I recognized God's voice inside my mind, calling me to fast psychotherapy: "Do not go, call, or write your psychiatrist or therapist for forty days."

I could not imagine my life without Dr. Ross and his wife, Jill, my therapist. As I considered fasting, I thought, *Surely, I will die.*

During the past ten years of my adult life, I had based my choices on my feelings. The last decade had found me tuning in to the voice of an inner child inside of myself. I will refer to this inner child throughout the book as C.J. (Child Jeanie). Behind the closed door of therapy, I allowed her to have a voice. Throughout ten years of psychotherapy, she had the capacity to act independently and make her own choices. C.J. and adult Jeanie were usually in conflict.

A small child approached me as we were leaving church that morning and handed me a tiny wooden ark. She said nothing as she placed the small cutout into my hand. Recently I'd learned that when the earth flooded and the rains subsided, the Ark came to rest on a mountain for forty days (Genesis 8:4–6). I pondered the huge boat, sitting on top of a mountain, waiting for the instructions of God.

I placed the tiny ark in a prominent place at home, allowing it to serve as confirmation: The voice I heard in church came from the Lord.

Surely my forty days would not reflect that kind of waiting and inactivity. I anticipated depression, loneliness, and anxiety. *Would I feel empty and alone without the weekly therapy I had grown accustomed to?*

As my fast began, nothing could have prepared me for the coming weeks.

I was captivated by my heavenly Father; His daily presence made me feel new. The depression and despair I expected never came. Instead, I enjoyed the pleasure of rest, the revival of joy, and the reassurance of His love and care for me. Not a day did I think about calling, writing, or running to my counselors of the past seven years. Visiting these two counselors, as you will see in my story, had become an addiction. Instead of fixating on my next visit, I found myself living each day in the moment. Never alone.

Jesus poured into me His peace along with His presence.

It was as if I was tasting a food I had never tried and thinking, *This is the best thing I've ever eaten.* I had been introduced to someone who made me feel more special and valued than I had ever known. I found myself pondering, *Could this be what I am made for? Has this Person loved me all my life?*

The songs I had sung about Jesus or written accompanied by my guitar were taking on a new meaning. Like learning a new language, I thought that this language must be love. All my feelings could be shared with my family, unlike the previous years in counseling. The past decade found me hiding half of my personality. For years, I had prayed to be whole. *Could this experience with Jesus be the answer to that prayer?*

Waiting took on a whole new meaning. I wanted to savor each day and live life one day at a time.

I attended my weekly Bible study on day thirty-six of my fast. A friend asked me about my weekend plans. "Jeanie, I'm attending a retreat in Chapel Hill, North Carolina, and someone had to drop out. Would you like to go in her place? Aqueduct Conference Center serves delicious meals and has a lovely outdoor setting. All your expenses will be paid. It will end on Sunday and the speaker is a professor from California. Dr.

Charles H. Kraft who will teach from his recent book, *Defeating Dark Angels*."

Personally, the subject didn't motivate me, but it sounded great to get away and enjoy time alone to journal and talk to God. My husband, Michael, gave his blessing, agreeing to hang out with our two youngest, Libby, thirteen at the time, and Kristofer, three.

Chuck Kraft and his wife, Meg, interacted with the fifty guests as though they were old friends rather than new acquaintances. His book provided fascinating material on the role demons play in a Christian's life. Dr. Kraft had used a method of kicking them out of the mind, will, emotions, and body that had imparted freedom to hundreds of individuals.

Over the weekend Chuck used volunteers to demonstrate the type of inner healing prayer that brought deliverance. Men and women were set free from unwanted habits, unwelcome thoughts, and undesirable behaviors.

We witnessed a prayer session between Becky and Chuck. Becky, a pretty woman in her thirties, soft-spoken and confident, carried a melancholy presence. During the dialog prayer with Chuck, we learned she led a healing prayer ministry in South Carolina. She and her husband, childhood sweethearts, had two boys before he became lost at sea on a pleasure trip with two of his friends. His boat never returned, and his body was never recovered. Never. Now remarried, Becky came to hear Dr. Kraft specifically, being familiar with his books and prayer ministry.

Chuck began, "Lord Jesus, in giving us authority, in Your name, to defeat dark angels, I forbid any outlandish behavior, as You reveal truth and expose the lies Becky has believed."

After Becky provided some history, she said, "I have thoughts about total strangers when they come near me."

Chuck responded, "What kind of thoughts?"

"I can hear someone talking and think, 'Get away from me! I hate you,' when in fact I don't even know them," Becky added.

I had never heard anyone openly discuss those types of thoughts, but they were familiar to me. Never questioning where the thoughts originated, I assumed everyone experienced them.

The prayer continued, sounding more like conversation. Chuck kept the dialog going with his questions while Becky provided answers based on what she heard inside her mind.

Dr. Kraft demonstrated hands-on intercession. He modeled how to listen to the person receiving ministry, while also listening for the leading of the Holy Spirit. He used questions that were brought to his mind as he prayed. The person being prayed for was free to interject any comments or issues they were dealing with. The sessions were nothing mystical or magical, but they just brought truth to light and exposed what the enemy had attempted to conceal.

On Sunday, February 7, 1993, I was still at the retreat, and the date came with no conscious awareness at the time that I had reached the fortieth day of my fast. I did, however, feel compelled to asked Becky if she would pray for me.

"Let's get the big guy," she responded. "We can all meet in the chapel after lunch."

We found Chuck and several others in a chapel that was small, quaint, and dimly lit. This sacred space contained a wooden kneeling bench and a large, open Bible lying on the nearby table. The comfortable sofa and chairs added to the ambience of the room. I was fine with everyone being there. As we began, all of us had the sense that we were on Holy ground.

Chuck began in his calm, strong tone of voice, "I take authority over this room and the legal spiritual right we have to be here. All spirits are subject to the Lord Jesus Christ and there will be no dirty tricks on those present or their loved ones. Any shenanigans, silliness, or mischief, dishonest activity or maneuvering, including yelling or outbursts of any kind, are forbidden."

Chuck explained he would ask me questions and I would answer according to what I heard in my mind. He explained that all demons are deceitful, but during this specific time they were under the authority of Jesus' name.

I felt calm and safe, without pressure in knowing how to answer.

Chuck began, "Spirit of fear, are you there?"

"Yes," I answered in a normal voice.

"What gives you the right to be here?" Chuck asked.

"We've been around since before her birth," Fear responded with my voice. "Jeanie's mother had been told she carried a dead baby because the doctors heard no heartbeat. I came into her mind and emotions, and no one ever kicked me out."

Dr. Kraft questioned, "What other spirits came with you?"

I heard myself respond, "Anger, anxiety, and deceit came too."

Taking time with each question to determine the demon's onset and legal right to enter, he called to attention more than twenty dark angels, including those responsible for shame, bitterness, hate, and lust. During the prayer dialog I felt no embarrassment. I felt cared for, known, and loved. This rescue took part for me, on my behalf, and yet, I never devised a plan. I simply wanted prayer. I never expected this amazing encounter.

Are you wondering what happened to the demons? Read on to find out.

Chapter 2
SHINE THROUGH ME

During the prayer session, all the demons were commanded into a box, which was sealed and sent to the feet of Jesus, as Dr. Kraft commanded. He spoke without theatrics, but with great authority. The seven other people joining me in the chapel were able to visualize what took place. Feeling clean, I knew these unwanted spirits were outside of me, unable to torment me any longer. No. Longer.

Dr. Kraft's gentle personality reflected an air of kindness. His spiritual gifts equipped him for powerful prayer ministry. I had never met anyone who prayed like Chuck. The timing of this encounter belonged to Jesus. It was perfect, and the experience brought to mind the verse, "for I know the plans I have for you.... plans to prosper you and not to harm you, plans to give you hope and a future." (Jeremiah 29:11).

As Dr. Kraft continued, his tone indicated that we weren't finished with our prayer session. "Jeanie," he spoke softly, reminding me of Dr. Ross. "We have another matter to take care of. Would you give me permission to speak to the little girl inside of you who has been wounded?"

Tears rolled down my cheeks. I knew he meant C.J.

"You are the only one who can see her and love her. Would you be willing to pay attention to her?" Chuck asked tenderly. "Your inner child has felt isolated and alone. She needs to feel loved and accepted by you. Can you introduce her to Jesus?"

Ten years before this conference, before Dr. Kraft and these prayers, I wanted nothing to do with an inner child. If she existed, no one else could see her, and I couldn't remember her. This little girl once lived in the past, forgotten. That part of my personality surfaced only behind the closed door of psychotherapy. Now, in answer to Chuck's question, I said, "Yes! I want to know her and love her. Yes, I want her to know Jesus will never leave her."

In 1965, as a ninth grader, I heard about a personal relationship with Jesus, during a church youth conference in Pennsylvania. It sounded wonderful, and I wanted it. I imagined that this Jesus would want me on His team, the way the athletic kids in school got picked for kickball games. I had gone to church my whole life, and I thought of myself as a good person. Our speaker in that huge auditorium said we could bow our heads and pray a prayer after him. Then the relationship would begin. Sounded simple. Only one thing escaped me: I didn't confess any sins. Unaware I had any worth mentioning, a spirit of pride inside me kept sins well hidden.

Now in the chapel with Dr. Kraft and the six others, I saw my sins. I recognized my own anger, unforgiveness, selfishness, and deceit. I wanted desperately to confess them to

Jesus. I then thought of the verse, "All have sinned and fall short of the glory of God," (Romans 3:23).

Also clear to me for the first time were the sins of others. I believed the lie that I needed to carry the blame for the sins of others, along with their guilt and shame. Without knowing, I had allowed the father of lies to operate in my mind, will, emotions, and body. Those lies included my distorted self-image, lack of self-worth, and self-destructive behaviors. I told Dr. Kraft that the enemy felt trapped as I confessed my sins out loud.

Chuck said, "I see a new expression on your face, Jeanie. How do you feel?"

Finding it difficult to describe the freedom I experienced, I reported what I heard the enemy saying in my mind: "So what! So, you rescued one. We [demons] are all over the earth, and you can't save all those who are demonized."

I will always remember Chuck's words, "This is one you no longer have."

The hours in the chapel passed like minutes. Chuck asked, "Would you like a hug from Jesus?"

"Yes!" I replied, expecting him to reach over and hug me. Instead, I felt the presence of my Father God holding me securely and safely in His arms. I heard Him speak in my thoughts, *This one's Mine!*

Making the sign of the cross with his fingers over each of my ears and eyes, Dr. Kraft prayed, "Lord, let Jeanie hear and recognize the sound of Your voice, as I anoint her ears to hear and her eyes to see You."

Even as I reflect on this prayer encounter, it's hard to believe that simply having someone pray aloud, addressing issues I once felt ashamed to speak of, could bring about such a dramatic change in my life. I was no longer in search of the Father—we had been introduced!

I left that small chapel a new person and with a memory I could never forget. Each year on February 7, I share my story of freedom with a group or individual, and I share the song God gave me, which you will find printed at the end of this chapter. To date, that covers nearly three decades.

Chuck Kraft and Jeanie at an Anaheim, California conference, one year after deliverance prayer in Chapel Hill, North Carolina.

Several days after I returned home from the retreat, my husband asked me to pray for him the way Chuck had prayed for me. Amazed that he wanted that prayer, I felt afraid that I would let Michael down because I didn't have the experience Dr. Kraft had. But remembering Chuck's teaching, I realized the power belonged to Almighty God and not to us. He taught us how to listen and pray for others around us. I never expected to apply this healing prayer to Michael. God used ten years of psychotherapy to prepare me for the rescue I have shared. God's story is much bigger than my own and demonstrates His faithfulness to His children.

"Shine Through Me"
Words/music: Jeanie Connell, February 25, 1993

I had sung about the Living Water,
I knew He hung upon a tree,
I had walked my life with Jesus,
And I believed I was truly free.
And then one day
God sent him [Chuck] from above
So I could see His tender grace and love.
I asked for prayer and His blessings flowed so free
And on that day, I knew Jesus had rescued me!

CHORUS: Now shine through me. Shine through me.
Let the whole world know, let Your whole world see.
Now shine through me, shine through me.
Let the whole world know Your love
As You shine through me.

Listen to this song at jeanieconnell.org/music.

Chapter 3
PROMISE YOU
WON'T REMEMBER

Although I had no memories of birthdays, or of interactions with friends and family before I was ten, after I got home from the retreat, I had a spiritual birthday, which became more important to me. Each year as I shared my testimony, it seemed I had a growing family within the body of Christ.

Well acquainted with my mom's mantra, "Promise you won't remember," I never considered the impact it had on my life. During ten years of counseling, I never shared it with any of the professionals who worked with me. Mom used this expression often, when she became embarrassed by her outbursts of words or uncontrolled anger. She would become intense, shake my shoulders, and ask for my promise that I would forget. She was hoping to obliterate evidence, like someone clearing material from a magnetic tape or disk.

When I entered psychotherapy and told her that I couldn't remember my past, she would say, "Thank God you can't remember." *Who says that?* I wondered. *Why?*

A favorite anonymous quote, "You don't know what you don't know," pointed to many of my early life experiences. I didn't know what caused my mom's extreme highs and lows. She died at age seventy-eight not knowing herself. I didn't realize I wasn't to blame for my dad's distance or his lack of affection. I didn't know my older sister, Barbie, resented me because my birth came fifteen months after her adoption, robbing her of an exclusive relationship with our parents.

I didn't know my younger sister, Kathy, would remain my lifelong friend.

Christmas in Flint, Michigan, for three sisters:
Barbie, 8, Jeanie 6, Kathy 2 years.

I also didn't know that my maternal grandfather had a sexual preference for children. Whether my grandmother knew about his perverted behavior...I don't know. Before I ever saw a psychiatrist, Kathy entered an in-hospital program in California for six weeks. Our parents flew out to babysit and Mom would repeatedly call the hospital asking about what

Kathy remembered. The staff finally had to ask her to stop calling.

My husband had a difficult time understanding my mom and a harder time trying to convince me that her behavior appeared unhealthy. The word "normal" refers to the typical, expected behavior we have seen modeled in our home. I grew up to regard Mom's outbursts of anger, imbalance of moods, and abundance of emotions as the norm. I had no knowledge of my mother's childhood relationship with her father. No one diagnosed Mom as a victim of incest or confronted her father with his unlawful acts. Mom loved her dad. They were close and, as his only daughter, she was the favorite.

She kept her dad's perverted behavior a secret, fearing that to expose his actions would be a betrayal. Living her lifetime in that denial, she remained unable to recognize any danger to her own daughters.

It would take a number of years before I could realize that Michael's conclusions about my mother were right. When Michael became part of our family, he too became familiar with Mom's mantra. The lack of trust that developed in their relationship chipped away at the state of connection they once shared.

My role growing up seemed to be keeping Mom calm. Dad, equipped with wisdom, appeared passive and uncomfortable dealing with his wife's emotions.

Barbie had a way of triggering an angry response in Mom, while Kathy could evoke a closer, more positive reaction, except when she spoke truth our mother couldn't handle.

My little sister, as a toddler, gave Mom a detailed account of Grampa's sexual advances toward her, unaware whether they were right or wrong. Mom responded with an explosion of anger, "Don't *ever* say those things about your grandfather!" Kathy remembers running to a closet to hide, feeling guilty and ashamed, as she took all the blame upon herself. It became her secret to carry from that young age through puberty. It would be following our grandpa's death that his secret sins as a child molester were revealed. Kathy's stay in the hospital returned her childhood memories that she had repressed. Confronted with Kathy's truth, and looking for validation, Mom broke the silence by tearfully saying, "I believe you because those things happened to me." Then, instantly transforming from vulnerable to defensive, she announced, "But I loved my dad! I loved my dad!" It was as though she were exposed and in jeopardy.

As an adult, discovering the truth of Mom's upbringing filled me with sadness for her. She remained stuck, holding onto what she wanted to believe about her father.

Mom, so much more than her invisible wounds, had a gift for cooking and being a hostess, welcoming guests and preparing incredible meals. As a loyal friend and loving mother, she considered her three daughters, their spouses, and all grandchildren to be top priority.

Both my mom and dad longed to conceive children. After eight years of waiting, they adopted my sister Barbie. Also, in common, my parents were musical. My dad had an amazing baritone voice. He and my mom sang in church choirs and loved singing with their friends as Mom played the piano by ear. Her fingers danced over the keys; she found such joy in singing and playing, much the way I do with my guitar.

Although I don't have memories of Mom tenderly taking care of me anytime I needed it, I do have one fond memory of her bringing me sliced bananas sprinkled with sugar and covered with milk when I became sick.

Mom expressed her love when she would take my sisters and me on shopping trips for new clothes and when we would enjoy lunch in fancy restaurants. Her happy mood convinced us we could buy the items we wanted, although within a day or so, she appeared stressed and regretted the money she'd spent.

Mom and Dad also loved to square dance and wore outfits that fit the occasion. Wearing that outfit seemed to lift her spirits.

Mom loved her girlfriends, never having a sister. And my girlfriends loved being around my mom. She listened well, offering generous and friendly surroundings. Where Mom had a wealth of emotions, Dad seemed devoid. I never doubted that he loved me, but I felt guilty for dreaming of a father who would call me *Baby*, or *Princess*. Hearing other girls talk about their fathers in those terms, I felt disappointed. Since my dad had been adopted and grown up as an only child, I don't believe he knew how to encourage that kind of father-daughter relationship.

Dad always provided beyond our needs, happier to give than to receive. He modeled integrity, and he loved to read. He liked things orderly, which was not easy with four females in the house.

All I really wanted from Dad was memories. Shared, happy, safe memories.

My book title reflects the words Mom wanted to erase that were laced with regret. Like toothpaste squeezed from a tube that could not go back in.

As a mother myself, I can understand what it's like to live with regrets. It's normal and natural to feel disappointment, even embarrassment, over our weaknesses. I've learned through experience that asking forgiveness is more helpful than demanding amnesia. We learn from others' mistakes as effectively as we learn from their strengths.

My mom and I shared something vitally important that neither of us was aware of. We both lived with bipolar depression. Undiagnosed, she never received treatment that could have made a significant difference in her thinking and emotions. Mom's mantra stood as a wall between my search for childhood memories and my promise to forget. My personal experience of a bipolar diagnosis is addressed in a later chapter. *You don't know what you don't know.*

In 1966, when I was attending Southwestern High School, in Flint, Michigan, my father took a job in Chicago, Illinois, we had to move, and my life turned upside down. Born in Flint, I loved my friends. My nickname, Gidget, originated from the television show about a teenager, played by Sally Field, short in stature and always barefoot. The TV character lived near the beach with her handsome father. On the show, there was no mom in the picture; the dad's role portrayed all you would expect from a perfect father.

Though my average height differed from that of Gidget, I went barefoot most of the time, which emulated her.

Secretly, I longed to be anyone's little girl, though this was not something I admitted or talked about. I wonder...*Do our secrets make us sick?* My thoughts of wanting to be taken care of like a child began as far back as my memories could take me. I looked for adults in junior high, high school, and even church who expressed the kind of love I saw reflected in movies and television shows. A parental type of love.

We attended a large Presbyterian church downtown. A friend and I sometimes played hooky from Sunday school, where our parents thought we were, and we would go instead to get a chocolate shake at the soda shop. Sometimes my older sister, Barbie, would join my friend and me as we spun around on the vinyl-topped stools in front of the counter. I felt invisible because my teachers did not even notice if I came. I guess I was trying to be a bit rebellious. I would have never missed choir though! I was in choir faithfully during all my years growing up, (even the years I couldn't remember) and I loved it. I even earned a gold pin for perfect attendance in choir!

Leaving behind everything familiar and adjusting to a new high school in Glen Ellyn, Illinois, I found one place that I fit: Young Life, a Christian organization for teenagers who gathered weekly to sing contemporary songs from a little brown book, watch laughable skits, and hear a short teaching from the Bible about Jesus. I first became part of Young Life in Flint. The summer before we moved, I attended Frontier Ranch, a Young Life property in Colorado, where teenagers from several states were making new friendships. I had no interest in dating but preferred being everybody's friend.

In 1968, after high school graduation, I attended Trail West Lodge, another Young Life property near Colorado Springs, Colorado, where I served with about twenty-five members of the college work crew. These volunteers from across the United States had been chosen to take on kitchen, dining-room, and cabin-cleaning duties while they also interacted with adult guests who financially supported Young Life.

I know during my eight weeks in Colorado I lost twenty pounds by eating nothing but Ritz crackers and drinking Diet Dr. Pepper. Despite my energy slipping away, I got up at night and did hundreds of sit-ups while the other girls were asleep in our cabin. One of the college guys on work crew came to my cabin trying to convince me to eat something. He even offered to feed me. I was starving for more than food; I hungered for attention.

When I returned home, my parents said almost nothing about my weight loss. I didn't want *their* attention, though, because I associated attention in my family with causing trouble or acting distastefully. Barbie had that role covered by smoking cigarettes and being boy crazy. Kathy held a unique position in the house by virtue of being the youngest. During this period, I became aware of how desperately I craved attention from others outside my family.

I did begin receiving attention from people outside my family at George Williams college. I was introduced to Michael Connell by my suite mate, Nancy, who was dating him at the time. She told me he had transferred from Ohio State University, where his only brother attended, and their dad played football. I was beginning to enjoy time with my suite mate and Michael, but I was interrupted by a family event…

While I was living in my college dorm, Mom came to pick me up on campus and we were getting ready to go on a shopping trip. We were interrupted by a phone call from my sister Barbie, who lived with my parents along with her little girl in my old room. "Please come home," she said sounding tearful and afraid. "If I didn't know better, I would think I was giving birth to a baby." Thankfully, my school was only 15 minutes away from my parent's home, and Mom and I headed home right away. In the time it took us to get there, Barb, who already had a little girl and was familiar with the pain of childbirth, had delivered a healthy baby boy, cut the umbilical cord, and called the ambulance. She must have felt so alone and afraid.

Mom and Dad adopted Barbie as an infant and loved her dearly. They could not, however, change the fact that her biological mom gave her away. This separation caused an emptiness that Barb tried to fill with unhealthy relationships. As I mentioned, she already had a little girl, who she had as a teenager. We all fell in love with this child. Her little girl was still a toddler when Barb became pregnant and remained in complete denial until she made the phone call to me at college.

As her family, living under the same roof, the pregnancy was easily concealed by Barb's normal shape, which was rather short and round. It broke Barbie's heart to have to give up her second child for adoption when she had lived a life of feeling rejected by her own biological mom. There was no room in the small Illinois house to bring in a baby, nor was anyone available to care for him.

After Mom and I got to their house, she took off in the ambulance with Barb. I stayed behind to greet my dad as he returned from work. When tragedy or trauma strike, we don't see it coming. In all the Kodak moments from this event that could have stood out, the look on my dad's face seemed the saddest. He loved Barbie. He loved his family. I couldn't imagine how he felt as a parent. There were no tears, only the look that held shock and disappointment. I also didn't know what Barbie went through in giving up her baby for adoption.

None of us knew what the future held in store for the son she had to give away.

"The best and the worst are the moments we recall" is a line from one of the songs I wrote.

Back at school, I remember some of the best moments that first year. I found Michael easy to talk to, kind, and smart. When he planned a trip with a group of friends to see his family at his alma mater, Ohio State University, he invited me along for the weekend since his girlfriend and my friend Nancy had a swim meet.

"Sure, sounds like fun," I responded.

Michael, his roommate, and I piled into his used car and took off for Columbus, Ohio. He showed enthusiasm as he gave me tours of the campus, the basketball court, stadium, and downtown, where shouts could be heard from students, "O-H" echoed by "I-O!"

That weekend stay with his brother, Bob, and his wife, Diana, would change the course of my life. The feelings I experienced were new to me. I felt warm inside and protected. Michael admired my long, auburn hair and my smile, and accepted my hippie lifestyle—bare feet, bell-bottomed jeans, and painted daises on my knees with plastic paints.

I admired his jet-black hair and dark glasses that gave him the studious look he deserved. So, I found myself attracted to him. Nancy found another guy to date, and she and I remained friends. I came to Columbus to be introduced to a college campus and discovered so much more. This reality is affirmed in the verse Proverbs 16:9, which says: "In their hearts humans plan their course, but the Lord establishes their steps." After graduation in 1970, when I moved to New Jersey with my parents, Michael and I began a long-distance relationship. I'm so grateful we courted during an age of snail mail, rather than text messages. Those letters remain a treasure to me. He introduced me to a world of athletics, and I introduced him to roller coasters. Not the kind in an amusement park, but the roller coaster of emotions that lived inside of me.

Although I didn't have many of my childhood memories, I do remember that during a chilly Christmas, Michael drove from Ohio to New Jersey to ask me to marry him over the holiday.

I found my boho-style wedding dress in a New York City boutique and wore Mom's Juliet cap, which she had worn as a bride, with fresh daisies. Feet usually bare, I put on cream-colored ballet flats for the momentous occasion.

Michael and I went from friends to more-than-friends, to long-distance pen-pals, to engaged with a diamond ring and three-foot stuffed pink and white giraffe. Michael knew how much I loved stuffed animals (I still love them!). My heart was so full that he included this child-like fun for such a sentimental moment. This gesture and many others enabled me to know that God chose Michael as the husband I needed. We chose each other.

On June 26, 1971, Michael and I married at twenty-one years of age after he graduated cum laude. Our wedding vows reflected the relationship that has lasted more than half of a century. We recited two scriptures. He read

> Love is patient, love is kind. It does not envy, it does not boast, it is not proud. It does not dishonor others, it is not self-seeking, it is not easily angered, it keeps no record of wrongs. Love does not delight in evil but rejoices with the truth. It always protects, always trusts, always hopes, always perseveres. (1 Corinthians 13: 4–7).

And my vow to Michael was:

> Where you go, I will go, and where you stay, I will stay. Your people will be my people and your God my God. Where you die, I will die, and there I will be buried. May the Lord deal with me, be it ever so severely, if even death separates you and me (Ruth 1:16–17).

A vow, a solemn promise, is what Michael and I proclaimed. A promise means giving an assurance to do something.

Chapter 4
BLACK AND WHITE

We honeymooned in the Essex House Hotel in New York City, followed by a week in the battlefields of Gettysburg. We were both eager yet nervous about our new beginning; I found him to be tender, gentle, and patient as I discovered the sexual side of myself, which had remained as hidden as my secrets.

There is no way to imagine what's in store for a marriage when you stand together so young at the altar of a church. The road ahead holds both delights and detours, rainbows, and rapids—all of which are unknown.

Our married life began in Middletown, Ohio, with us living in the upstairs of an old brick house owned by Mrs. Smuckers (like the jam). We had to walk up two flights of cement stairs outside and another carpeted staircase inside to get to our entrance. We would push together two twin beds for greater intimacy. We were finally married and able to make our own decisions, including being responsible for our finances.

One of those decisions was both of us working. I found a job in Middletown Hospital admitting patients, while Michael began his YMCA career. We both took an active position in the community, including a leadership role in the local Young Life club. With a group of volunteers from our church, we held a weekly morning breakfast for teens. We also took them on planned weekend ski trips. My husband had a history of working with young people. They were his comfort zone, and he spoke their language.

When I shared my first original song in Middletown, with a small women's home Bible study group, I discovered that not everyone had melodies and lyrics in their head. I learned the value of any song I wrote could only be determined by me. Just me.

We moved to Auburn, Indiana, in 1973, and it seemed the perfect place to have children. The town was small, the streets were safe, and when Michael transferred to the YMCA in Auburn, he already knew one of his coworkers. We were embraced by the community, and we felt loved. That love helped when I miscarried in the summer of 1973. Thankfully I was able to give birth to Kyle in 1975. Being a mom proved to be the greatest joy I had known. Although I tried to work part time for our church, I would tear up just thinking about anyone else taking care of this adorable human being instead of me. So, I took care of him—and loved every second of it. When he turned six months, I wrote "K.C.'s Song." Here is an excerpt:

> *He has funny little giggles, he has trouble holding still, he has a bald little head and a stubborn little will. We have very*

special feelings. We have a whole lot of love. We have a precious little baby, sent to us from above.

In 1976, we moved to Lowell, Michigan, where Michael directed a branch of the Grand Rapids YMCA. We rented a house that had a swimming pool in back and, on occasion, when the owners gave permission, we could enjoy a cool dip.

In the summer of 1979, I canned peaches and tomatoes while waiting to deliver the next baby I carried. On August 30, our only daughter, Elizabeth Eileen Connell, entered the world, named after Michael's mom. I remember the first moment I held her in my arms, whispering, "We got a girl. We got a girl." Thrilled to have both a son and a daughter, we were grateful and satisfied.

Kyle adored his little sister and remained on call for her every need. All the neighbors came to visit her. She didn't lack for love or attention. I wrote her first song at six weeks of age.

"Elizabeth, Elizabeth"

Elizabeth, Elizabeth, why won't she smile at us?
Elizabeth, Elizabeth, why won't she play with us?
Elizabeth, Elizabeth, what are we gonna do to show you we love you?
Elizabeth, Elizabeth, why won't you look our way?
Elizabeth, Elizabeth, don't turn your head away.
Elizabeth, Elizabeth, what can we do or say to have you look our way?

We all think you're adorable! We all think you're stupendible!
We all think that you're wonderful, but it would help if you'd
be more adaptable!
Elizabeth, Elizabeth, look she's gonna smile! Elizabeth,
Elizabeth, hang on, it takes a while,
Elizabeth, Elizabeth, she's finally learned the game!
Elizabeth, she knows her name! (LOOK, she smiled!)

Taking up jogging for the first time in my life, I quickly shed my baby weight through exercise.

I ran my first 5K race and became depressed if the weather kept me indoors.

Our family of four moved to Shelby, Ohio, in 1983, where we made close friends through the YMCA and our Methodist church. I started a youth choir with teenagers.

Kyle had excellent elementary teachers. His best friend lived next door to our red rented house with the large front porch. In winter months the frost on the inside of our bedroom closet kept us freezing. I remember sitting on the floor register vent in our dining room where the hot air came up, trying to warm my hands. The backyard had a perfect hill for sledding, and our kids and their friends took full advantage of it.

With so much to be thankful for, I'm uncertain why the eating disorder from college days returned with a vengeance. Looking back, I think starving myself gave me a greater sense of control that I longed for. I did not feel out of control as a mom, but I felt like I had no control over when we moved from one state to another. Leaving behind friends, churches, doctors, and schools left me feeling like an outsider often. I wanted to belong. I was always new, and I felt like I needed to prove myself, which was difficult. Somehow, what I put or didn't put in my body seemed like something I could control. Anorexia and bulimia, though, went undiagnosed until 1984, when the eating disorders began taking control of my life. I felt guilt and shame for lying to Michael and throwing up in secret. This habit became an addiction, which soon required professional help. The thinner I got, the fatter I felt. I had a distorted body image. Throwing up, purposefully emptying the contents of my stomach, became my ritual if I ate anything sweet. Eating a donut without the opportunity to throw it up resulted in a meltdown. I feared gaining weight and felt like a failure.

Michael knew a young woman with a counseling practice in Shelby, and he asked me if I'd like to make an appointment. I went, and I felt safe as Debi listened. I talked…mostly about food. This hour did not resemble a friendship because Debi didn't reciprocate. The sixty minutes existed only for me.

I certainly didn't consider my eating habits to be a form of mental illness.

I had never talked with a counselor before, yet in college, I majored in psychology. I enjoyed trying to understand the way people thought and why they behaved the way they did.

Before going further in my story, it will be helpful to establish the difference between a counselor, a therapist, and a psychiatrist.

Merriam-Webster's Dictionary defines the terms in the following way.

- "Counselor: a person who provides advice as a job: a person who counsels people //a marriage counselor."[1]
- "Therapist: an individual specializing in the therapeutic medical treatment of impairment, injury, disease, or disorder, especially; a health-care professional trained in methods of treatment and rehabilitation other than the use of drugs or surgery."[2]
- "Psychiatrist: a medical doctor who diagnoses and treats mental, emotional, and behavioral disorders: a specialist in psychiatry."[3]

Questions like, "What is your earliest memory?" were wasted on me. As I've mentioned, my earliest memories began somewhere after ten years of age. That didn't seem strange to me. *We don't know what we don't know.*

In Shelby, Ohio, I reached the lowest weight I would ever be. Lying on my back at night, I could feel my bones extending as though they were more prominent than my flesh.

At times my frame frightened me as silent tears rolled down my cheeks. Other times I felt proud to be several sizes smaller than usual.

Before I had even had twelve months with Debi, in 1983, we moved to Spencer, North Carolina, which cut off my time with her and the progress I was making on my mental health journey. The move for Michael's career, though, was more than just another promotion. The Salisbury YMCA, located equidistant from Raleigh, Charlotte, and Winston-Salem, became Michael's new mission field, and he was flourishing.

We were excited about the move because we were able to purchase our first home with three bedrooms and two bathrooms, which each had a bathtub. We considered these amenities luxury! We had a separate dining room and living room, plus a family room with a fireplace where we hung Christmas stockings from the mantel and sat on the large brick hearth. Both the front and back yards were large, with lots of green grass and trees. We lived across the street from North Rowan Elementary School, where Kyle and Libby attended. Beside and behind our house were Libby's childhood friends. A tribe of little girls.

Having moved every three years up to this point, there seemed no reason to believe we would stay in North Carolina any longer. We never imagined this house would be our home for the next eleven years.

Spencer, North Carolina, 1993
Our family: Michael, me, Kyle, Libby, Kris

Many significant life events were going to be packed into that decade. Both good and bad, including nine years of psychotherapy that would, as I mentioned in Chapter 1, would become my addiction.

"Black and White"

Music/lyrics: Jeanie Connell

Don't be angry when I'm honest, don't be troubled when I frown,

I am finding there are lots of ups to follow all my downs.

I'm beginning not to fear the pain or the feelings from the past,

God is teaching me that just like growth, healing won't happen fast.

You can stand beside a mirror trying not to look away,

But you'll never see the inches that you're growing every day.

When you skin your knee and clean it up, you can try to watch it heal,

But the process goes so slowly, changing not by how you feel.

There is good and bad. There is black and white.

We will both succeed and fail, knowing wrong and right.

If you love me let me fall apart, if you love me let me grow,

If you love me don't hang on too tight, in loving me you'll know

When I need you to be very close, when I need you to be strong,

And I promise you my loving heart whether you're right or wrong.

Listen to the song on Jeanie's *Roots* CD,
available at jeanieconnell.org.

Chapter 5
JESUS, DO YA EVER CALL ME "BABY"?

Most days in our new home I was parenting Kyle and Libby, now five and ten. I enjoyed working as a teaching assistant, preparing meals, baking, and playing guitar. Exercise came easy—bordering on obsession—and was the highlight of every day. It kept me "safe." Safe from unwanted weight gain.

I had some desire to read, and *Your Inner Child of the Past*, by Hugh Misseldine, caught my eye in the local Salisbury library. It kept me spellbound as I devoured every page cover to cover. Finishing, I hurled it across the room like a frisbee and muttered, "Rubbish!" I was angry that I had taken my time to read it, and equally angry at the author's ideas. *I certainly didn't have an inner child inside of me!*

My thoughts were interrupted by a phone call on that day in 1984. There were no cell phones in those days. When your phone rang, you had to run to pick up and answer before the final ring or your answering machine kicked in.

The familiar voice of my sister Kathy said, "Honey, you need to locate a Christian counselor because we are both dealing with issues related to our childhood. We grew up in a family thinking it provided a normal, healthy environment. It didn't."

Kathy and I were kindred spirits. My younger sister knew me as well as anybody. When she called me, she had recently returned from spending six weeks in a California hospital's psychiatric program, which I mentioned earlier. Although with Kathy, the staff had focused on her weight fluctuation, her fellow patients were dealing with other psychological issues. As Kathy interacted with patients there, some of her childhood memories surfaced, including the years of child sexual abuse suffered at the hands of our maternal grandfather.

Though I still struggled with obsessive thoughts about food and distorted body image, my personal story held no similarity to Kathy's. I thought to myself: *I hope she doesn't think I had similar experiences to hers. I'm sure I would remember if there had been any child sexual abuse in my past.*

Kathy's therapist had drawn a parallel between her eating disorder and mine, saying when more than one member of the family struggles with anorexia or bulimia, it usually indicates childhood trauma.

Even though I didn't like the direction of her thoughts about my childhood experience, I did take her advice in seeking professional counsel. Michael found a Christian psychiatrist a couple hours away through the recommendation of a friend.

My doctor, who I'll call Dr. Williams, was an older man close to my father's age with a similar physical appearance. He seemed to be well established in his profession, judging from the copies of his book lining his bookshelf. He prided himself on working with patients who struggled with eating disorders.

Was I afraid of food? Yes. Did I have a clue what to expect in talking to a psychiatrist? No!

During our initial appointment, my nonexistent inner child appeared. That was the first time —but it would not be the last.

"I'm glad you came to see me today," Dr. Williams began. "It's okay if you would like to lift your head and look at me. You remind me of a little five-year-old, sitting on your legs with your long hair framing your face," he continued.

I returned a sweet, innocent smile, sitting very still, unprepared for Dr. Williams's follow-up. "Would you like to be my red-headed daughter? I've always wanted a little girl with red hair."

From that moment, my life changed.

Those words were not only unexpected but became planted in the deepest recesses of my mind. An unspoken desire, never brought to the surface. I could not even imagine my own father speaking those words to me.

I looked around his office as he swiveled his large desk chair around to face me. Apparently, he could see a part of me that I had kept hidden away. A secret part of me, unsafe to share. Strangely, instead of feeling exposed, I felt safe. I had no desire to acquaint myself with this part of my personality. However, I wanted desperately for someone else to discover her. To know and care for her.

Arriving home from my appointment, I immediately wrote a note to Dr. Williams containing two questions: "Did you mean what you said? Can I really be your daughter?"

My first psychiatrist! Someone much more important than me with initials after his name. I trusted him to know what I needed. Again, my mantra went through my mind: *You don't know what you don't know.*

Dr. William's handwritten response arrived in the mail a few days later: "Yes, you can!!"

Every week for the next eighteen months, I walked into his office, the door was closed, and we spent the next sixty minutes talking together. Being listened to that intently felt like a dream come true and worth the money I had to pay. I felt secure. I began to realize that my childhood had gotten lost. I had no idea what caused it to be forgotten. *Where had this part of my personality been hiding? How could it exist inside of me?*

Some who have read my story have questioned the methods of this psychiatrist. For them, it raised red flags. Only in retrospect, however, could I recognize the ways this doctor used his position of power to tap into my unmet wants and desires. Believing this man could provide me with safety and protection—like that in a father-daughter relationship—set me up to be confused and to believe in a lie. We are only set free by the truth, as the following scripture tells us: "Then you will know the truth, and the truth will set you free" (John 8:32 NIV).

Let me clarify that when I was seeing Dr. Williams, my own father and mother were alive and well. My dad had always proved to be a good person. He loved me in a distant sort of way. Though he was smart and well read, I never experienced the closeness in the relationship with my dad that I felt with Dr. Williams.

Looking back, I can't condone Dr. Williams' methods of treatment. I would warn anyone in a similar situation to get out and seek help elsewhere. That said, people are not just good or bad; they are made up of both.

No one asked me to keep my new role as my psychiatrist's daughter a secret, but it felt too fragile to be shared. The risk in telling someone could shatter my dream-come-true. Because Dr. Williams had told me I could be his "daughter," I believed that I was special—more special than any other patient—and those beliefs took precedence over uncovering any memories from my past. I just wanted to be loved and cherished.

During those eighteen months in treatment with Dr. Williams, the thirtysomething part of me searched for evidence of my childhood. We rarely spent the hour in adult communication. In one of those sessions, Dr. Williams would impart one of the most critical suggestions anyone had given me to strengthen my marriage.

"Jeanie, do you and Michael pray together?"

Surprised by his question, I answered, "No."

He may as well have written it on a prescription pad. His words were clear and concise. "You need to start. And when you are praying, hold hands." *What possible difference could it make to hold hands?*

Returning home that day, I told Michael exactly what Dr. Williams had said. We both received his instruction as being essential to my health, and we began praying together immediately. Little did we know that this small prescription would become life-changing for us throughout our marriage. We also learned the importance of holding hands. It seemed that most times when we would agree to pray, one of us didn't feel like saying the words. We had never held hands, so doing so was awkward for us. The best we could manage was to have our fingers barely touching. Gradually, it got easier.

As for the relationship with my doctor, I shared most everything about my life while he shared almost nothing, other than the fact that he had a wife and five children and believed in Jesus.

While under his care, we attended a church that had a master life course. In that course, we learned to memorize Bible verses—a new experience for me. Absorbing God's Word in two-hour classes became satisfying. After refreshments were served, I headed downstairs to the nearest bathroom to empty my stomach. A battle raged inside of me. I didn't trust myself to fight the battle nor did I believe I wanted to win. My mind played tricks on me. *If I win the battle over anorexia/bulimia, I will be fat and unlovable.*

Although I faced a battle, my behavior and feelings for Dr. Williams were useful in that they gave me many clues about the little girl I couldn't remember. Compared to my adult persona, she appeared selfish, scared, and secretive. Therapy became a costly habit of kicking off my high-top tennis shoes (a staple of my fashion choices in the 1980s), curling up on Dr. W.'s cozy sofa, and talking about food. Child Jeanie needed therapy to find her voice. Taking off my shoes helped me feel more childlike. On no occasion would C.J. communicate with my parents or my family. She felt separate. As I've mentioned, I made her acquaintance in the professional realm of therapy.

At the end of every appointment with Dr. Williams, he would come and sit beside me on the sofa, let me snuggle beside him before leaving, and then he would help me lace up my high-tops, which further made me feel loved and cared for like a little girl. I faced the most difficult part of each week knowing I had to go home and wait an entire seven days before seeing him again. In his presence, my feelings became vulnerable and exposed. I would have the two-hour drive back home to hide them away and transition into the adult wife, mom, and friend people knew. Changing from C.J. to Jeanie, while replaying recent conversations in my mind, led me deeper into the lie that Dr. Williams could be the father I longed for. My weekly habit had grown into addiction, which remained a subject we never addressed behind the closed door of therapy.

After I had spent a year or so with Dr. Williams, he invited me to be part of a small support group facilitated by his wife, who I'll call Beth. To my knowledge, she had no initials after her name nor training to lead such a group. She showed kindness to each of us and demonstrated good listening skills.

My memories of this group were more focused on one of the members, rather than Beth: a young woman who had struggled with agoraphobia an anxiety disorder in which the person fears the outdoors, perhaps resulting from panic attacks. Her diagnosis seemed more serious than mine, and I felt jealous of her relationship with Dr. Williams and his wife. I somehow got the impression she had a much longer history with them than I did. I drew the conclusion that she got more attention.

I gave little thought to the group, which lasted only a matter of weeks. Later in my life, after I watched a movie on television about a woman with agoraphobia, I realized the great degree of depression, and even post-traumatic stress, involved in her diagnosis. When I received treatment from Dr. Williams, though, my only thoughts concerned myself, without consideration for what the other members of the group were going through.

Following the termination of the group, during my weekly appointment with Dr. Williams, I remember prodding him to anger. I sensed his growing frustration to uncover the source of my feelings, along with the dilemma of addressing it, as he blurted out, "If you were my child, I would have turned you across my knee by now!"

Whispering in my quietest voice, almost hoping my doctor wouldn't hear me, I said, "That's what I wanted."

The atmosphere in the room changed instantly. His exasperation and annoyance evaporated as he responded with a confused question, "You wanted me to spank you?"

I felt embarrassed, even ashamed.

He seemed relieved to know what I was thinking.

My reality and illusion collided.

The thoughts in my mind stacked up like a ten-car pile-up on the freeway. *Why? Why couldn't I have what I wanted? Why would I want a spanking in the first place? Had Dr. W. lied to me when we first met? Why did he say I could be his red-headed daughter? Would I have trusted him without the lie?* I would never know.

The message I received loud and clear that day: Dr. Williams would never be the father I wanted him to be—the father he promised to be. A father who set down rules and disciplined with love. I had no memory of that in my own home. I desperately wanted memories I didn't have.

I longed for the discipline talked about in the following verses: "My son/daughter, do not despise the Lord's discipline and do not resent His rebuke, because the Lord disciplines those He loves, as a father the son/daughter he delights in" (Proverbs 3:11–12).

Then in Hebrews 12:9a NIV, it says, "Moreover, we have all had human fathers who disciplined us, and we respected them for it."

Behind the closed door of therapy, I recognized my childlike thinking and behavior. It didn't trouble me if I could hide it from my family and friends. I felt that no one could really understand the relationship between me and my psychiatrist. No one.

I continued my weekly appointments. The next one began with the usual exchange of hellos.

Then I learned something I never knew. Dr. Williams had made a phone call to my mom (with my permission) in which she reported, "When Jeanie was a small child, she would come in crying after playing with her sister Barbie and say, 'I want to be adopted too!' as though her only hope to receive love and attention could be adoption."

Dr. Williams found it fascinating that the natural-born child felt less special than the adopted daughter. Clearly my parents went out of their way to make Barbie feel wanted and special.

Uncovering a true story from my forgotten childhood felt like a big deal.

*8/10/52— Older sister Barbie and me
playing in the sand. I'm two years old.*

I don't remember talking very much about my mom or my dad. Most of my friends were unaware that I had an older sister. I didn't see a need to bring her into the conversation.

Most of the memories I had with Barbie were not happy ones. In our adult years, we began to appreciate each other as sisters and to accept each other's differences.

The therapy sessions with Dr. Williams went into my collection, to be kept like favorite recipes. Each time my appointment ended, as I have mentioned, my psychiatrist would tie the laces on my pink high-top tennis shoes and join me on the cozy sofa, where, as I leaned into his broad shoulder, another memory would be made.

I expected another session, eighteen months into my therapy, to end routinely. Wrong.

Sitting on the sofa, Dr. Williams said, "Jeanie, it's alright if you want to put your legs over mine while I sit beside you."

C.J. had no memories of being held in anyone's lap, so the invitation sounded tempting. Knowing Dr. W. (as she called him) could not be her father, the offer seemed innocent enough.

Then…it happened. With my legs still flung over his, he asked me a question: "Did you intentionally touch my genitals with your hand?"

I sat frozen, uncomfortable, and embarrassed, unsure I understood the full importance of the word "genitals." *I was cuddling like a child, and he was talking like an adult.* I felt fear and wanted to protect C.J., who accompanied me behind the closed door. I sat silent, wanting to leave, and not knowing what to say without creating greater awkwardness. I knew I had done no inappropriate touching, accidental or otherwise.

This experience deeply troubled me. I felt unable to discuss it with anyone. If any part of my father-daughter illusion remained, it shattered that day like a broken vase beyond repair.

One week later I made my final appointment with Dr. Williams. At the close of the hour he asked, "Jeanie, would you like to sit in my lap today?"

As I declined his invitation, "No, thanks," I appreciated this rare occasion to have C.J. agree with me. Maybe she and adult Jeanie were not as separate as I once thought.

Although I decided to stop going to him for therapy, I hoped my psychiatrist and I could still maintain a friendship.

After so many years of starving for attention, I came to a place where I wanted to cry out to God for sound mental health. The first step in facing any addiction is admitting there's a problem and asking for help.

My simple prayer began, *Jesus, would You heal me? I have been so afraid to ask because I feared the future. Now, with Your Word inside me, I'm ready. Thanks for listening. Amen.*

The combination of weekly appointments with my psychiatrist and memorizing God's Word left me with the certainty that God had chosen to heal the eating disorder I had lived with.

Well into an unremarkable day, I noticed something remarkable. None of my thoughts centered on food.

From high school years through adulthood, my waking thoughts were food, calories, and exercise. Trust me when I tell you the absence of those thoughts resembled a miracle to me.

A Chinese proverb says: "The journey of a thousand miles begins with a single step." Could this lack of obsessive thoughts about food be my single step? As years turned to decades, I would never again be held captive to fears regarding my body. I asked and God answered when He led me to the following verse: "Until now you have not asked for anything in My name. Ask and you will receive, and your joy will be complete" (John 16:24).

I have never denied the good news of God's miracle. However, I would soon discover anorexia/bulimia to be only a symptom of another diagnosis.

Going from my habit of weekly appointments to zero communication with Dr. Williams left me feeling abandoned, even though I had made the choice. I hoped my psychiatrist would want to witness the change in my life, so I drove two-hours to his home both without an appointment and without Michael's knowledge. His wife greeted me, "I'm sorry, Jeanie, Dr. Williams is not available."

Disappointed, his wife and I chatted for a bit before I returned to my car. My elevated mood dropped dramatically. The opportunity to see my former doctor presented a closed door, and I had no way of knowing that God had plans to open it again years later.

Asking for help wasn't easy, but the more difficult part involved letting go and moving on.

I still felt determined to meet the father who disciplined, the one to whom I could be special. Persisting in my search to find him, I knew he had to be out there somewhere.

"Jesus, Do Ya Ever Call Me "Baby"?"
Words/music: Jeanie Connell

Jesus, do Ya ever call me "Baby?" Do Ya ever think that maybe I could be that someone special to You?

Jesus, will You wrap Your arms around me, let me feel Your love surround me?

Adoration undeserved, yet so true.

Don't be taken by my grown-up nature; though I know I act responsibly,

Underneath it all is someone crying; "Please just love me!"

Jesus, are You close enough to hug me? Once I thought You were above me.

Can Your loving really satisfy me?

Don't be taken by His God-like nature; though you've known Him as the "King of Kings,"

Underneath it all is Someone crying, "Please, just trust Me."

Jesus, are You close enough to hug me? Can You really be my Daddy?

Do Ya ever call me "Baby?"

Listen to this song on Jeanie's *All I Have to Share* CD, available at jeanieconnell.org.

Chapter 6
FLASHBACKS

No longer under a psychiatrist's care, my memories remained hidden. I clung to the following verse and prayed it often: "The secret things belong to the Lord our God, but the things revealed belong to us and to our children forever, that we may follow all the words of this law" (Deuteronomy 29:29).

I asked the Lord to help me remember anything I needed to be whole.

Alone in our house, with the kids in school and Michael at the YMCA, I suddenly felt ill. I sat down at our kitchen table thinking, *What's happening?* I reached for a mixing bowl as a precaution, feeling strangely sick to my stomach.

I began to see pictures in my mind that were not familiar to me. How could they be familiar? The figures had no faces. There were disconnected voices that made no sense. Imagine random puzzle pieces landing in your lap and none of them fit together.

In the pleading voice of a small child, I could hear myself say, "Don't hurt my sister Barbie! What are you doing? Who are you?"

Ending the bizarre episode, which lasted several moments, I felt violated in some way. Out of breath. Confused. Certain this event would never happen again. Sadly, the unsettling flashbacks returned.

After this first experience, I could count on Michael to be beside me each time they surfaced. Thankfully neither Kyle nor Libby was present as I appeared to throw up emotions against my will. The memories always came in the voice of a child: "What are you doing to me? Who are you?" The feelings were strong. Seeing no faces made it a mysterious, unsolved puzzle. Breathless and shaken after each episode, I would feel shame clinging to me like unwanted slime.

Following these unexpected, involuntary, recurrent memories, I would try to reassure Michael that I would be okay. "It's over. We will get past this."

Disturbed, he replied, "Jeanie, it's difficult for me to see you like this. What could be causing it?" Neither of us had the first clue what brought on the flashbacks or how to make them stop. Things were changing. We prayed together daily, asking God to intervene.

I contacted Dr. Williams to see if he could shed any light on the subject. We disagreed about my going to see him in person. I felt like it would be moving backward rather than forward to end up in his office again after finally breaking the visits off. He wrote me the following letter:

October 2, 1986

Dear Jeanie,

I received your letter and disagree with you strongly. I do think that you need to continue to see me. I am glad to know that things are moving along, but I don't think that you are ready to cancel your appointments yet. If you do so, you do so at your own risk of having another outburst or similar outbursts of what you had recently. Please listen to what I have to say and decide that you cannot be your own psychiatrist.

Yours in His service,

Dr. Williams

Referring to the flashbacks as outbursts, Dr. Williams felt he could help me if I were his patient again. I never shared with Michael the reason I discontinued my treatment with Dr. Williams. However, we both agreed that the door had been closed, even though we were getting desperate for another door to open.

After another week of these episodes, which left me feeling unbalanced and exhausted, we heard about a counseling center about an hour from home.

As Michael and I sat in the waiting room, a woman on staff came over to take my history. "Hello, Mrs. Connell. I need to gather some insurance information from you. What is your current address?"

I felt the flashback approaching. The involuntary memory appeared like a seizure as I cried out in the voice of a child and spoke regardless of who could hear. I could see the woman watching as the unwanted episode ran its course. Within minutes, she directed us to a nearby in-patient psychiatric facility.

What a relief! I thought. *Help at last! Someone will diagnose what's wrong and be able to fix me.*

When Michael and I arrived at the well-kept, modern building where psychological problems were dealt with, the staff checked my bag for hangers and pointed objects. Asked to name the President of our United States, I thankfully answered correctly. I could only assume they were testing the soundness of my mind.

I left my husband in the lobby while I got checked in. A nurse completed a physical, even though my issues were related to my mind, not my body. While I sat on the edge of the exam table in a paper dress, a tall, bald, soft-spoken man walked in and introduced himself. "Hello, Jeanie, my name is Dr. Ross. Could we talk a little bit so you can tell me what's going on? How old do you *feel* right now?" It seemed a strange question, but my answer seemed stranger.

"Ten," I replied.

I think it's important to determine if you can trust someone when you're wearing paper and feeling ten. Being in my early thirties during that initial meeting, I trusted handsome and kind Dr. Ross when he said he would be my psychiatrist. He assured me we could talk more the following day.

Though difficult for both Michael and me, we said our goodbyes. A nurse ushered me into a room with two twin beds. One belonged to my roommate, who had attempted to end her life. I missed my husband and felt lonely. I'd never spent time in a psychiatric hospital. During the night I heard someone yelling.

As I heard them yelling words I couldn't understand, I wondered: *What's wrong? Why are the other patients here? Is this the right place for me?*

After finally dozing off, I woke up with a flashback approaching. Calmly, I got up and headed to the nurse's station. One of the staff on duty stepped away with me to a private area. I tried to prepare her for what she would experience, not wanting her to be frightened. I explained that I would see images in my mind, people with no faces. "I may cry out or say things that don't make sense, but it won't last long, usually less than five minutes. I appreciate you staying with me. You don't have to do anything, I will be okay," I reassured her.

I hoped I wouldn't freak her out. She handled it well, and I returned to my room.

Life felt so uncertain. My surroundings were unfamiliar. If flashbacks could enter my life with no warning, what else did I need to be prepared for?

Getting back into my twin bed, I considered putting notes on the wall beside me in case I became unable to communicate the next day. My fears were irrational.

Viewing my hospital stay as a low point in my life, I felt guilty for needing help.

For years I had struggled with migraine headaches and lost entire days with my husband and children due to the pain. I was sure I was going to lose more time with the family I loved.

The hospital had a good smell, except the room where patients smoked and watched television. It felt more like a nice hotel than a hospital. Every day I met with about fifteen other patients and doctors, who met in a room, sitting in a circle. We listened to each other's stories and shared our own when we were ready. With Dr. Ross in the circle, I felt safe there. I liked getting to know new friends. Our sunny cafeteria had good food choices. The payphone in the hallway allowed patients to make and receive calls. This facility had a relaxed and friendly atmosphere. I felt thankful to be there to receive help. Michael and our kids came to visit. Several friends that I worked with from Libby's school also came to encourage me.

Knowing the hospital dealt with mental health issues attached a stigma to it. The following is an excerpt taken from an article from the Mayo Clinic's Website

Stigma is when someone views you in a negative way because you have a distinguishing characteristic or personal trait that's thought to be, or is, a disadvantage (a negative stereotype). Unfortunately, negative attitudes and beliefs toward people who have a mental health condition are common…

The article goes on by sharing the following tips to cope with stigma:

> Get treatment.
> Don't let stigma create self-doubt or shame.
> Don't isolate yourself.
> Don't equate yourself with your illness.
> Join a support group.
> Speak out against stigma.[1]

As patients, it was easy for us to feel misunderstood, so our counselors encouraged us to discover that we were brave. The puzzle pieces on my imaginary table still didn't fit together. I remained convinced that recovering my past childhood memories would make me whole.

The flashback that occurred on my first night in the hospital would be my last. Dr. Ross, Michael, and my friends all agreed that returning home would allow me to resume outpatient treatment with a doctor I trusted. Dr. Ross agreed to continue our professional relationship, and I hugged him goodbye. I felt fragile and looked forward to my first appointment with him outside of the hospital.

My psychiatrist gave me a test run before I was able to check out completely. I spent the day away from the hospital with Michael and the kids, then returned to spend the night. The following day, after one week in the in-patient facility, I returned home for good.

I wrote the following song to remember and pray for my new friends at the hospital. Like kids you meet at camp, we were all different, but came together for the same reason: to get well.

"Charter Mandala Hospital"

September 1986, dedicated to thirty-six new friends I met
in the hospital

I will sing when I feel lonely,
I will sing when I feel blue,
But each time I'm singing this song,
I will think only of you.
I'll remember all your faces,
I will hurt for your pain,
I will pray for your wholeness
That will come in Christ's name.

Don't forget all your tomorrows,
Though they're right or maybe wrong,
Let them throw you toward your Father,
In His arms where you belong.

Chapter 7
PSYCHIATRIST NUMBER TWO

Nervous and somewhat timid as Dr. Ross ushered me from the waiting room into his private office, I felt certain that C.J. would make an appearance.

"How are you feeling, Jeanie?" he began, not having seen me since my week in the hospital.

I responded softly, "Okay," while looking around my new psychiatrist's office. There were large bookshelves and impressive medical degree certificates. He had a large wooden desk with a chair that swirled. C.J. wished she could trade places and spin around in his chair. I carried on adult conversation. "How is everything going with you, Dr. Ross? Are you busy at the hospital?"

"Thank you for asking, Jeanie, but our time together is not about me," he responded kindly.

"Michael and I recently returned from Myrtle Beach where some friends offered us their condo to relax and take walks on the shore," I reported. "But..." Lacking courage, I stopped.

"What is it?" my doctor inquired.

"I miss the hospital, Dr. Ross. Is that a bad thing?"

"That's perfectly normal, Jeanie. That's why we are meeting together for a while. As long as you need to talk with me, I will be here. You can drive up to the office and we will schedule some time," he concluded.

C.J. and I both loved the sound of that.

"Dr. Ross, the lady that taught my education classes at the hospital had a different last name than yours. She's pretty, with a soft voice, and treated some of the other patients. Is she married to you?"

I was unsure if I could ask that type of question, but he indulged me and answered, "Yes, Jill is my wife."

Dr. Ross never filled silences with words unless they were necessary. He knew how to listen.

He could give his patients medication, but I never wanted that. I didn't think I needed it. I saw my psychiatrist for talking. And a hug.

"Dr. Ross, I thought I had a normal childhood. We all went to church. Now I'm not so sure what I believe. I feel confused about a lot of things. A couple years ago my younger sister, Kathy, went through an inpatient hospital psychiatric program and uncovered memories of her childhood. Our grandfather had a sexual preference for children," I reported without emotion. "Since I have no memories of my childhood, I never assumed that my early years were anything but happy."

"Jeanie, do you remember anything about your mom's dad?"

"Not before age ten. After that I remember him kissing me

by blowing on my cheek and making a squeaky sound, while his scratchy face made me want to pull away. He led a boy scout troop and dressed up like Santa Claus for the Detroit Thanksgiving Parade. There were strange toys inside his big desk and a workshop in his basement. He would do pull-ups on the steel bar without his shirt on," I reported. "I didn't like it there."

I continued: "My sister Kathy, his favorite, went with him to the creek behind our house. Sometimes I went to the creek too, beside the railroad tracks. I didn't like it there either. Grampa talked too much and didn't listen. I didn't feel loved or close to him. I remember when he died, and I didn't feel sad. The funeral home smelled bad, and it upset my stomach."

I don't know what made it feel safe to talk to Dr. Ross. My words poured out nonstop. Maybe it was his office or his voice. Maybe it was the way he listened, like he really cared. I knew our time together would end with a hug, and I trusted I could return a week later. The bond between us continued to grow. But progress seemed agonizingly slow.

Fast forward a few months…My parents were coming for a visit, and it troubled me. I found it difficult to understand the longing I had for Dr. Ross to take care of me, knowing my own God-given parents were coming to spend time with me and our family. I had no memories of my parents that mirrored the ones I had with my psychiatrist. Adult me and C.J. were at odds.

Ambivalent and fearful, I took an overdose of pills. I didn't take enough to end my life, but I did take a triple dose of my migraine medication, which did make me woozy. I was seeking attention and nurturing from my doctor. I confessed what I had done to Dr. Ross. He called Michael and sat with me in the patient waiting room while my husband drove the sixty minutes to collect me. The waiting room looked like a large living room; there were lamps, sofas, and cozy chairs. I wasn't expecting the question from my doctor: "Jeanie, were you trying to kill yourself?"

"No way! It never crossed my mind!" I answered indignantly. "I wanted you to see the hurt on the inside." *It didn't feel like enough to come to Dr. Ross's office once a week. I couldn't cry. I didn't know how to communicate what I was feeling. I was trying to show him.*

He responded softly, "I understand, but there are other choices you can make when you are hurting or afraid. Choices that don't pose a threat to yourself or others."

How far would C.J. go to gain his attention?

Did I have secrets locked inside? Was it possible to have an inner child from my past make decisions in my present? Aside from Michael, no one knew about this uncharacteristic behavior. I never expected to repeat my mistakes, but I couldn't see into the future.

Left: Kyle and Libby, my daughter, at seven years old;
Right: me at seven.

Chapter 8
LEARNING THE HARD WAY

I usually looked forward to my hour with Dr. Ross, but I dreaded the end when C.J. would have to transition into a responsible adult for Michael and our two kids.

Where food once occupied my thoughts, therapy had become my obsession. *What would we talk about? What would I wear? What could make me more special than my doctor's other patients? Why couldn't I remember the past and uncover my memories?*

The hug we had established became the precursor for walking out of the office. When our sixty minutes were up, he would rise from the swirling chair to signal we had reached our goodbye. Never more than one hug, although I asked. And each week, I made a memory.

One day Dr. Ross said, "Jeanie, I don't hug all of my patients goodbye."

Shocked, C.J. asked, "Why do they come?" My psychiatrist had no explanation, only a chuckle.

Aside from the hug, I believed that Dr. Ross could help me. He concentrated on people's minds, so I felt sure my memories would surface for him. It never occurred to me that new ones were being made.

I journaled and prayed, asking God to show me what could have caused me to blot out the past. Finding no answers to make me whole brought deep discouragement and depression.

I usually entered my doctor's office with a long list of questions. Dr. Ross told me that most of the answers would be found inside myself.

"How will you know this (or that)?" C.J. would insist.

His confident reply came: "You will tell me."

Hmmpf. I will have to think about that.

I knew he couldn't read my mind. But he listened like someone searching beside me for buried treasure. I knew he cared about discovering my past.

"Jeanie, is there a reason you are facing the wall today instead of looking at me?" Dr. Ross asked. "The braid in your hair looks very pretty," he continued.

Could C.J. have been any more obvious in wanting him to notice and compliment her, or make her feel special?

My response came, spoken in C.J.'s childlike tone of voice: "Dr. Ross, how do you make a memory?"

His only answer was mild-mannered laughter. He showed a gentle and sensitive temperament toward C.J., who frequented his office more than my adult persona did. I grew to love the sound of his laughter. It allowed me to feel like I had pleased him.

At other times, C.J. felt anything but happy. Feeling sad or stuck, I didn't recognize those feelings as depression.

If a key becomes stuck in a lock, you can't force the key out or take apart the lock on your own. You need a locksmith who is trained and experienced to deal with the problem.

I saw Dr. Ross because he'd been fully trained and was experienced in dealing with people like me—People who were sad or stuck.

During an evening appointment my psychiatrist began with a question. His tone of voice, as if he were addressing a little girl, got C.J.'s attention. "What's wrong?" he inquired with sympathy.

I always believed Dr. Ross could see and speak with C.J.

Instead of appreciating his kind, compassionate tone I responded with anger, "What's wrong with me? Why can't I make things right, Dr. Ross? Why can't I remember?"

"Jeanie, you have to give it time," he replied calmly. It seemed that the louder I became, the quieter his voice grew.

At the close of the appointment, I could tell he had a concern for my sullen mood. "Jeanie, is there anything else we need to talk about?"

I had received my hug. I recognized my time to leave. Not expecting this night to be any different from any other, I walked out the door. How. Wrong. I. Was.

Walking past my car in the parking lot, I kept going with no destination in mind. I felt lost inside, even though my surroundings were familiar. I ended up alongside an extremely busy interstate with cars whizzing past me. Ambling along with my head down as the night grew darker, I gave no thought for my safety.

Suddenly, I noticed a large house away from the highway. Without thinking, I wended my way through tall grass and stones and approached the front door, not knowing who or what awaited me. I knocked and a very kind woman invited me inside to use her phone—this incident happened well before everyone had cell phones.

I called Dr. Ross's office, asking him to return my call and leaving the woman's home number. Without waiting, I thanked this stranger and headed back down the interstate in the opposite direction. I wasn't thinking rationally. I wandered aimlessly with no notion of my destination.

I refused a couple offers to give me a ride, wanting only one person to come to my rescue: Dr. Ross.

Without my knowledge, he did return my call at the house where I had stopped. The woman described my state of mind to him as confused and reported that I'd been walking down the expressway.

Meanwhile, Michael became concerned since he hadn't heard from me for hours. He found a phone number for Dr. Ross.

As I traipsed off the highway looking for a payphone, I felt so relieved when I called his office a second time and heard his voice. "Dr. Ross, I wanted you to come and rescue me," said C.J., who surfaced at will.

"Jeanie, I'm your doctor. The only thing I could have done for you is call the police."

Well, that seemed harsh! Did he even care about me?

My psychiatrist continued in a matter-of-fact tone of voice, "Please have Michael call me when he finds you."

Panicked, I replied, "Michael is coming?" Feeling disappointed and equally relieved, I asked, "How will he know your number?"

Slightly irritated, he responded, "He found it once, and I'm sure he will find it again!"

I lived in my own world, unaware of those I inconvenienced or frustrated. I could only view the disruption I caused my husband or my doctor from my perspective. Everything was about my needs. I felt like a child running away from home, seeking to test her parents' love for her. *Will they love me enough to come after me? They'll miss me, I'll show them.*

Aimlessly, back on the two-lane road near the doctor's office, I noticed someone driving in my direction. I recognized Michael as he got out of his car. "Babe, are you okay? I've been so worried about you!" He threw his arms around me with such strength, reassuring me of his love and concern. He held me tightly as my arms hung limp at my side like a rag doll. I felt only the emotions that had led me down a busy expressway alone, sad, and abandoned.

Michael called Dr. Ross as instructed. "Jeanie, your doctor wants to know if you want to go to the hospital tonight. It's okay if you do, Hon."

"No, I just want to go home with you and forget about tonight," I answered. Michael seemed relieved and reported to Dr. Ross that I had declined the offer to be admitted to the hospital.

I truly did want to forget the whole experience, including Dr. Ross's heartless lack of concern in finding me. Sadly, the following morning presented C.J. with a new mission of kidlike behavior. It's normal to want attention from parents. At times, children think they have to go to extremes to garner special interest and care. And honestly, sometimes that is what it takes.

Relentless in seeking Dr. Ross's notice, C.J. saw an opportunity by returning to his office building to collect the abandoned car from the night before.

With Michael at work and our kids in school, C.J. gave no thought before putting the plan into action. When I say no thought, I mean NO THOUGHT.

Deciding to ride my bicycle fifty miles in 90-degree heat did not fall under the category of wise choices. Giving no consideration to my lack of biking experience or level of physical strength, I took off without water, Gatorade, or staples of any kind. This plan had *disaster* written all over it.

Twenty minutes into the ride and too late to turn back, I recognized my poor judgment. As sweat poured off me, I had no idea how the pedals were turning as my energy level dropped to zero. The bicycle seat induced pain as my bones felt glued to the plastic. The saddle next to my gluteus maximus muscle, too narrow, lacked padding and became extremely uncomfortable the longer my ride continued.

Twenty minutes from my destination, a gas station appeared like a mirage in the desert. I had no money with me. By this point, all I wanted was to be able to sit down on *anything* except a bicycle seat and breathe. Everyone seemed to be staring at me. My beet-red coloring and gasping for breath should have provided me with a clue as to the source of their curiosity.

I found relief sitting next to the gasoline pump because my legs, feeling like rubber, would no longer hold me upright.

As I was hyperventilating, I called Dr. Ross's office from a payphone expecting at least some concern for my well-being. He never came to the phone. No one at his office expressed any interest whatsoever. No response. *Why was I paying these people?!*

My plan for attention resulted in no positive outcome.

Meanwhile, at the gas station, God watched over me, using the good deeds of a middle-aged couple who offered me a ride, loading my bike into the trunk of their car. I didn't get their name or where they came from, but I still give God the credit for their kindness.

I'm not sure it occurred to me to thank Him. God, that is. After all, He's invisible. The Bible says He loves us and will never leave us, so I figure He did a good job.

When I arrived at Dr. Ross's office, I went inside to be certain he had no interest in seeing me. This was confirmed by the girls I'd become acquainted with at the reception desk when I inquired, "Does Dr. Ross know I'm here?"

"Yes. We told him", one woman replied.

My bright-red face could hardly be ignored, but my doctor's lack of interest left me with no option but to head back home in my car with my bicycle in the trunk.

One more unsuccessful attempt at gaining attention. *I'm a failure. I don't deserve to be loved.*

Arriving home, I explained the day's events to Michael. After a hot shower, he took me out for a spaghetti supper. As we sat in a soft booth, he could have launched into a speech about what a boneheaded thing I had done. Instead, he showed me nothing but kindness. Grace. I felt undeserving, knowing I'd always remember his gesture of concern. Expecting judgment, I was shown only affection. Grateful for my husband but still unable to recognize how my actions were affecting him, I'm not sure I thanked God for our marriage, let alone for Michael's kindness.

C.J. inside my thirty-five-year-old body gained momentum. Unable to talk things out, she did an excellent job of acting out her feelings and fears.

After a typical sixty-minute therapy session with Dr. Ross, I ranted about never having enough time together. The louder I got, the calmer and quieter my doctor became. He knew how to counteract my meltdown: "Jeanie, you know I have tender feelings for you."

Feeling his concern, I made a memory that day from his choice of words.

Author Sarah Young has written a popular devotional titled *Jesus Calling*. On January 8, she writes, "Though I have all Power in heaven and on earth, I am infinitely tender with you. The weaker you are, the more gently I approach you. Let your weakness be a door to My Presence. Whenever you feel inadequate, remember that I am your ever-present Help. Hope in Me, and you will be protected from depression and self-pity."[1]

I wanted to believe that, by placing my hope in Dr. Ross, I could be protected from depression. I hoped that by exposing C.J., I might gain a tender response from my doctor. I was deluded.

He couldn't read my mind or unpack my distorted thinking. He was only slightly older than me, but my delusion led me to believe that Dr. Ross had the age and wisdom to be the father I longed for.

After my outburst concerning lack of time, my psychiatrist agreed to a four-hour session in his office.

The $400 appointment failed on several levels. I became weary of hearing myself talk, though Dr. Ross stayed attentive to the end of the marathon, and my bill to the insurance company brought my sessions to a halt for a month. *Why must I always learn the hard way?*

Were the long appointment and my bicycle ride debacle sufficient to teach me a lesson? No. Sadly, no. All kids must learn through their own failures in life, even when there's someone telling them how to avoid pitfalls. Sometimes we simply must experience them ourselves to absorb the truth.

Chapter 9
WAS I SEXUALLY ABUSED?

During ten years of psychotherapy, I never considered myself to have a split personality. Did my doctors? I don't know. We never discussed it. In fact, I don't remember anyone putting labels on me, except PTSD—Post-Traumatic Stress Disorder. I tried to diagnose myself from various textbooks. I didn't hear the term dissociative amnesia until years after my therapy began. I know this disorder is not caused by any type of brain injury, but rather, it relates to early trauma.

As I've said, my thinking and behavior looked entirely different behind the closed door of the therapy room than it did in my everyday life. I very seldom in those ten years shed tears during counseling, whereas I considered myself wealthy with emotions at home, especially relating to my husband. Strangely, I had seen Michael shed less than a handful of tears in our entire fifteen years of marriage.

As I uncovered C.J., I gave that part of my personality the freedom to express itself. It never failed to embarrass me or get me into trouble.

Not long after the bicycle incident, I came up with another bright idea. I became curious to know what Dr. Ross would do if I refused to leave his office at the close of my scheduled appointment.

Similar to the way kids test their parents' resolve on rules and limits, I wanted to find out.

Before I left for this appointment, I remember saying a prayer as I knelt by our kitchen table: *Lord, please let this plan work out okay. Help me to follow through. Amen.* I might as well have prayed, "God, please look the other way while I do whatever I please. Amen."

My expectation? Attention.

On occasion, Dr. Ross had to finish with another patient while I waited for him to enter the waiting room and invite me back to his office. Finding me there once he called me "Sleepyhead." Whether it was a silly nickname like "Hotdog" or a pat on the head, I interpreted it as a fatherly gesture. The kind of remark or gesture I wished my own dad would have made.

Other times he explained that in running late he had arranged to have his final appointment of the day with me. I felt special.

The evening of my bright idea, Dr. Ross called me in from the waiting area, and we headed straight back to his office. It never entered my mind that he would be seeing other patients after our session ended.

Unlike during our previous, standard sixty-minute sessions,

when I sat across from my psychiatrist talking face to face, on this occasion I reclined on the cozy sofa. Dr. Ross sat in his chair that spun around and tried several times to cajole me into conversation.

Because I felt nervous about putting my plan into action, I let the minutes tick away. I thought it was best to remain silent and wait.

After more endeavors to coax me into dialog, my doctor explained that he would use the session to catch up on his paperwork unless I changed my mind. "Jeanie, it's your choice to talk or not to talk during your allotted time."

Soon, my allotted time concluded. The moment I dreaded had come. His words were kind as he encouraged me to gather my belongings and put on my shoes: "Jeanie, it's time to go."

I stayed curled up on the sofa as if superglue were holding me there. Then I matter-of-factly announced, "I'm not leaving, Dr. Ross. I don't want to go."

Slightly irritated, he said, "You don't have a choice. Your scheduled time has expired." This rigid tone I had never heard before.

Like a rally in a ping-pong game, our "you-will, I-won't" exchange continued a short time before I realized that I had pushed my doctor too far. He spoke again from his swivel chair, which was now directly beside me: "Jeanie, this isn't acceptable. It's time for you to leave. Your appointment is over." His face conveyed frustration.

He made his point and I clung to mine. I had no idea what

to expect or what outcome I hoped for. God had ignored my prayer. In over my head, I couldn't turn back. As might have been predicted, the scene went from bad to worse. Dr. Ross walked out of his office.

Oh no! Oh no! Where did he go? Is he coming back? I'm in BIG trouble.

Still on the cozy sofa, I did not have a plan in place. With C.J. calling the shots, I jumped off the sofa and hid. There were very few hiding places in Dr. Ross's office. I slid under his big desk and scrunched up as small as possible. My head buried in my chest and trembling with fear, I remained as visible as the desk itself.

The door opened and Dr. Ross walked in and gathered my purse, shoes, journal, coat, etc. He gave me no direct eye contact as he turned and went back out the door.

Terrified, I could feel my heart beating *thump-thump, thump-thump! What's next?* Staying as still as a statue, I hoped to remain invisible.

My doctor came through the door a second time with a look I had never previously seen on his face. No words were spoken. He walked directly in front of me and grabbed hold of my wrists, giving no option for me to wiggle free.

I'd never had occasion to realize his physical strength until he pulled me to a standing position that day. He seemed taller than I remembered, and I'd never witnessed this expression on his face. I knew I had caused his anger. From the first moment

I met my psychiatrist, I only wanted to please him. There were no words to describe how awful I felt.

He dragged me through the hallway past one office after another as, humiliated, I begged and pleaded with him to let me go. Every doctor and patient in the building had a full view as I continued to appeal to his compassion. "Pleeeease let me go Dr. Ross! I have learned my lesson. On my honor I will never do anything like this again in my holy life!"

Completely deaf to my words, showing no emotion, he carried out his mission to remove me from the place I had considered safe.

My embarrassment escalated as we reached the front reception desk. He brusquely let go of my wrists like a hot poker, and shame and remorse covered me while people in every direction stared. Treating me as if I were invisible, Dr. Ross turned away, accompanying his next patient to his office as though nothing had happened. Nothing. Had. Happened.

My belongings were in a pile on the floor. Trying not to make eye contact with anyone, I put on my shoes and jacket to head outside.

Darkness had fallen, providing a hiding place for me inside my car. Unlike the inside of the doctor's office, this offered quiet; there were no human beings to stare in my direction.

Emotions bottled up within me found a voice as I began to scream...and scream...and scream. The wailing, loud and long, came from deep down inside me, yet thankfully no one heard. Every cell in my body filled with shame. I realized I wanted nothing to touch my arms, legs, or any part of me. Something traumatic had happened in my safe place, and I carried the blame and guilt. C.J. could not be trusted. Dr. Ross saw the little girl inside of me. I felt violated in a way I couldn't understand. Endless screams continued to escape through my mouth until my throat rendered me speechless. Worst of all, I had disappointed the one person I wanted to please—my psychiatrist.

With the familiar payphone nearby, I wasn't confident I could get out of my car and alert Michael that I would be late. *Could I ever tell him what happened?*

I understood my responsibility for my actions, whether C.J. or Jeanie. As a people-pleaser, not a rule-breaker, feeling small and violated, I doubted I could ever erase the memory of this horrible night. I could never imagine I would share it in a book for all to read about. Too ashamed and embarrassed to tell Michael what had happened immediately, I knew in God's time, Michael would know the whole story.

The following week I returned for my regular scheduled appointment with Dr. Ross. *Had I compromised our doctor-patient relationship? Would he ever want to see me again?*

Dr. Ross never asked me how I felt when he forcibly removed me from his office.

I never told him how I felt that night or mentioned the meltdown in my car. I only wanted reassurance that he still cared about me.

The conversation began with Dr. Ross: "Jeanie, I treated you just like I would have treated my own daughter last week. That behavior is called passive-aggressive."

Instantly, his words were engraved in my mind, making another memory. *Like. His. Daughter.* (I didn't fully understand the term passive aggressive. I would look it up later.)

My doctor continued, "Is there a question you would like to ask me?"

I responded quickly, "Yes. Do you love me?"

"That's not the question I meant," he said. "Do I forgive you?"

Obediently, I replied, "Okay. Do you forgive me?"

"Yes, you are forgiven," my doctor announced.

C.J., still pondering the thought that I had been compared to his daughter, was filled with joy. Nothing else mattered. The hour ended with our customary goodbye hug, and I never devised a plan to purposefully disobey him again.

My closest Bible-study friends seemed concerned about my growing dependence on my psychiatrist. I reasoned that they couldn't understand; they had never dealt with similar issues.

Janice, a friend from the mountains in North Carolina, had a different viewpoint. She was a trained therapist and we met during a Christian conference. Months later, she mailed me a book by Jan Frank titled *A Door of Hope*. It told the story of the author's experience of sexual abuse and listed the symptoms in adults who have been sexually abused as children and who do not remember. Repressed memories, not a familiar term to me, seemed to be telling my story and describing my treatment. Here is a summary of what Jan Frank says in her book.

Symptoms of Child Sexual Abuse in Adult Survivors

1) Depression; mild to severe
2) Anger; displaced to someone or something else
3) Fear/anxiety; often unexplained
4) Guilt/shame; can't feel forgiven
5) Difficulty in close relationships; lack of trust
6) Repeated victimization; often taken out on self
7) Shut-off/overcontrolled emotions
8) Sexual problems; including lack of sexual desire or exaggerated acting out
9) Low self-esteem; extremely poor self-image

Additional symptoms include migraine headaches, stomach ailments, pain of unexplained origin, eating disorders, sleep disorders, flashbacks, memory blocks.[1]

Jan had a quote in her book by David Peters, author of *Betrayal of Innocence*, who was well acquainted with the subject of abuse: "Research has shown that as high as seventy percent of women have no conscious awareness of a molestation that occurred in their past."[2]

After I shared the information in this book with Michael, he said, "Jeanie, are you a victim of child sexual abuse? You have every symptom on the list!"

We mutually decided I would show the book to Dr. Ross and get his input. During my following appointment he riffled through the pages and looked at me surprised. "Jeanie, I've been treating you as a victim of child sexual abuse since I met you."

My response: "Why didn't you tell me?"

Dr. Ross gently replied, "I thought you knew."

He thought I knew. *We don't know what we don't know.*

I questioned how I would ever get well at this rate, when my doctor knew things about me that I couldn't figure out myself. Healing felt entirely too slow! Too slow.

Chapter 10
ALWAYS IN A HURRY

After one year of working with Dr. Ross, I wondered if I could speed up the process by working with someone who professed to know Jesus Christ.

My close friend from the school where I worked told me about a faith-based hospital program in the Dallas, Texas area. The psychiatrists and therapists on staff were recognized for the books they authored. Paul Meier, M.D., and Frank Minirth, M.D., were respected in both Christian ministry and mental health circles.

I couldn't imagine being an entire plane ride away from Michael and our two kids, then seven and eleven. Another concern included the high cost of the in-hospital stay.

At my friend's urging, I continued praying about the idea. God began to open doors. Between Michael's insurance at the YMCA and my own school insurance, the cost would be covered. Then our small church congregation offered to pay my plane fare to Texas and back. Teachers from my school promised to spend extra time with Libby. My husband considered me brave to want to follow through with the plan.

It didn't come as a surprise to Dr. Ross. He knew I considered the pace of my healing to be entirely too slow.

Knowing God loved me, I believed He made a way for me to go to this hospital in Texas. I continued writing songs as He spoke to me through the language of music.

Before I left for Texas, Michael had a chat with Don Frank in California, whose wife, Jan, authored one of the books I mentioned earlier, *A Door of Hope*.

Having taken a similar journey with his own wife, Don said, "Be prepared that things will get worse before they get better."

"I appreciate your thoughts, Don," Michael replied with confidence, "but we have been through the worst of it. I'm sure Jeanie and I have weathered the storm."

Those words were spoken by a man completely unaware of the *hurricane* on the horizon, about to pose a threat to all he held dear.

One of my favorite doctors on staff in Texas, Chris Thurman, Ph.D., wrote *The Lies We Believe*. Leading our support group, Dr. Thurman shared his version of the Tortoise and the Hare. It got me thinking and inspired a song. My husband and I both needed patience with the process. We hoped and prayed we could reach the end of this journey soon.

Each patient in the Texas hospital adhered to a tight schedule from morning until bedtime. There was a time to wake up, a time to take a walk (per doctor's recommendation), a time for support group, and a time for individual therapy, plus mealtimes.

Before my eyes were open in the morning either Dr. Minirth or Dr. Meier showed up to read my chart. I don't recall much communication at that hour.

I do remember seeing the carts in the hallway that delivered medication in little cups. No one got as much as an aspirin without a prescription from their doctor. I presented my choice clearly: No drugs.

I had no problem with what the other patients needed. Looking back, I felt my choice protected me, afraid that if I took medication, it would label me. My mother didn't believe in medication. I hardly knew her to take an aspirin. It would be many years before my viewpoint changed.

Speaking of viewpoint, I had serious issues with the young, pretty, confident, in-charge therapist assigned to me. Her name was Cynthia Spell, and she called the shots, which I didn't care for. She seemed self-assured, unlike me. She looked healthy, while I struggled on several levels. Cynthia was single; I, married with two kids, could not see what we had in common. She could come and go as she liked, something else I envied.

Concluding that she made money from talking to me, I decided to make her job as difficult as possible. It would take some time to knock the chip off my shoulder. She appeared too perfect. Picture perfect.

"Hey, Jeanie, I'm Cynthia. I'm going to be your therapist while you are here at the hospital. I'm looking forward to getting to know you," she said with her Southern accent. "I'm sorry I won't be around this weekend since it's Labor Day. I will be stopping back after the holiday." She spoke her words with extra syllables, reminding me of an Alabama friend in Young Life.

"No apology necessary!" came my sarcastic reply. "Take your time, I'm fine without you," I jabbed.

Our initial days of getting acquainted were slow. And then came the day my pretty therapist walked into my room without her air of confidence. Her focus had evaporated. *That* I could relate to.

I had never seen Cynthia close to tears or had the opportunity to empathize with her. Right before my eyes she turned human, vulnerable. Our relationship changed that day.

From then on, I looked forward to our conversations. We were bonding as we met together.

Once, during my free day at the mall in Texas, I spotted her with someone who looked like a possible boyfriend. The young man was giving her an innocent hug. At our next session I told her what I saw. She seemed uncomfortable that I recognized her.

I've found that those who work in the field of mental health want to know as much as possible about their patients, while they want their patients to know as little as possible about them.

I attended group therapy, also daily with a brave group of individuals whom I grew to love and respect. I looked forward to seeing this circle of friends and enjoying the openness among us as men and women. Our group contained a pastor, a surgeon, a teacher, a student, and a future counselor. All walks of life and all acquainted with brokenness. I longed to unearth any childhood memories that had gone untouched.

One patient in our group brought out the worst in me, bringing to the surface emotions of jealousy, anger, irritation, and more. She seemed to be manipulative, and that infuriated me. Staying in my seat, aggressively directing my words toward her; I manifested my feelings loudly and clearly as I demonstrated intense anger.

I could never forget what happened next.

Everyone in the group sat silent while I erupted like a volcano. Then one of the therapists stood up and announced in an authoritative voice, "Everyone leave the room now! Please go back to your rooms, including you, Jeanie."

They canceled group! No one ever cancels group! I wasn't finished.

In a short time, Cynthia and a male therapist came to my room, trying to get to the bottom of my outburst. I had transformed from powerful into timid. I felt small. "I never wanted you to cancel group," I confessed. "I thought you wanted me to express my feelings. Isn't that one of my goals?"

"Jeanie, where have you seen that type of anger?" Cynthia asked.

"That's the kind of anger Mom has," I admitted.

Cynthia spoke to me calmly, "Jeanie, when your mother erupts with that kind of anger, it's called rage. You can learn how to express anger that doesn't frighten or hurt others."

I felt sad, thinking I had disappointed Cynthia. I felt

ashamed. I didn't feel adult. I knew C.J. remained alive and well. Group therapy resumed the following day as usual. No more outbursts from me. I didn't want the kind of anger my mom had.

The following week Cynthia gave Michael a call in North Carolina. "Hello, Michael, this is Jeanie's therapist. I wanted to touch base with you. How are you doing?"

"Oh, I'm fine," he responded. "It's been a pretty good day. The YMCA keeps me busy."

"Well, that's not exactly what I meant," Cynthia explained. "I'm wondering how you are holding up after all the years that your wife has been experiencing depression and trying to unlock memories of her childhood."

Michael says that her phone call became a turning point for him. He remembers her call from Texas as being the first time anyone had asked about him. He remembers hundreds of times when friends and family asked about me, offering help with meals or our kids, inquiring when I might return home.

But that day, when Cynthia specifically asked about him, he realized he had been walking a unique journey of his own. A journey with his own issues, challenges, and fears.

When he put me on a plane to Texas, Michael became a single parent overnight. While keeping up his normal work schedule at the YMCA, he became responsible for Libby and Kyle. Libby's long, brunette hair needed tender loving care to tame the curls. A teacher at school offered to put it in braids each morning if Michael would send a brush and hair bands.

He eagerly accepted.

Michael's letters to me included stories of spilled molasses in our food pantry and Kyle's less-than-perfect grades, but he always encouraged me to concentrate on getting well. I would never tire of hearing him call me brave.

I felt guilty for leaving my family, worried what other people in our community thought, and I felt selfish for putting myself ahead of their needs. I expected to miss Michael and our kids. I left little prizes for them, like a treasure hunt, along with messages on a cassette. The idea backfired when Michael informed me that hearing my voice only drew attention to our distance, and we decided to withhold the tapes.

My private room in Texas resembled a hospital more than a hotel. It had a single bed and a private bathroom. Period. Adequate, but nothing fancy.

I didn't expect to miss Dr. Ross. I placed a call to his office, and he returned it when I had no scheduled activities. I missed hearing his voice and going to his office each week. "Hi, Jeanie, how is everything going?" he asked.

The adult spoke to Michael and other family members, but C.J. surfaced when talking to Dr. Ross.

"It smells the same here in Texas as it did in your hospital."

Chuckling, he asked, "Is that a good thing?"

"Yes," I responded. "I miss you, Dr. Ross, and I don't know how I feel about working with a woman." I chattered on as though he were sitting across from me in his swivel chair. "I've made lots of new friends here, and one day I got a headache and threw up. I have a therapist named Cynthia, and I didn't like her at first, but now I do."

"A very accurate report, Jeanie. Are you doing what they ask you to do?"

"Yes, Dr. Ross. And thank you so much for calling me back and...I love you." The three little words just popped out. C.J. hadn't planned to say them.

Just as quickly my psychiatrist echoed, "We love you too, Jeanie."

Thinking: *Who were "we?" The rest of the staff at his office? I knew he didn't plan to say those words.* Wanting to remember their sound forever, I would replay them in my mind a hundred times. Always in a hurry for everything else, but never in a hurry to leave Dr. Ross.

It would take something drastic to separate us.

"Always in a Hurry"

Words/music: Jeanie Connell, 1986, Wysong Hospital, Richardson, Texas. Inspired by Dr. Chris Thurman.

Always in a hurry to get there, always in a hurry to start.
Always in a hurry to get there, always in a hurry to start.
My friend said, "Who won the race between the tortoise and the hare?"
I know the answer, yet I can't believe that he made it there.
What was his method as he set out to win the race?
Consistency, hard work, and a very slow pace. But I am*
What can I do if I see that my heart's like the little hare?
I desire to win the race, I am strong, I can win it fair.
Lord, I want to give up all my own plans and hopes at all cost.
In gaining more of You, I cannot be lost. But I am*
Lord, change my heart and set it on the highest mountaintop.
You know just how far up I can go till I need to stop.
I commit my heart to You without fear, believing You care.
I claim Your wisdom, trusting You to be there.
'Cause I am always in a hurry to get there, always in a hurry to start.
*Always in a hurry to get there, always in a hurry to sta-a-art.

Listen to this song on Jeanie's *Roots* CD,
available at jeanieconnell.org.

Chapter 11
BEHIND A WALL

The announcement came over the seventh-floor PA system: "Anyone wanting to attend church this morning, meet at the front desk, and we will load up the van." As far as I knew, all the patients had permission to take part. I chose church over sitting in my room.

I liked the young pastor and made two new memories that Sunday. The first memory was after the service when the preacher approached me and gently lifted my chin, saying, "Jesus loves you and wants you to lift up your head." His personal touch felt like that of Jesus Himself.

The second memory took place in the ladies' room, where I hid underneath the countertop, hoping no one would discover me. Only annoying C.J. would do something like that. I didn't understand the behavior, didn't mention it to anyone, and never returned to the Texas church.

A word about hiding: Maybe you have a memory of your own about hiding somewhere as a kid. It comes naturally to children. They hide in the circular clothes racks, in small dark hutches underneath a staircase, even behind the folded rugs hanging in a department store. Hiding is part of the kid experience. That said, it seemed outside my normal nature at that time.

A room in the hospital known as the quiet room piqued my interest. It was a place designed to express anger. I hoped that if I entered it my suppressed anger might surface.

The walls were soundproofed, there were boxing gloves on the floor, you could scream without disturbing anyone. I asked Cynthia if I could go in.

Picking up the puffy, black boxing gloves, I hit the wall a few times. Nothing. I gave screaming my best effort but felt more anger when I left than when I entered. The lack of tangible results left me disappointed and frustrated. My memories continued to elude me. *Where were they? Who could steal them? I had no clue who to be angry with. Or did I?*

Talking with Cynthia during our routine private session, I remembered something from my past. It didn't feel all that dramatic at the time, just a piece of my life that I knew to be true. It was like finding one of your belongings under the bed, out of sight, that suddenly surfaces.

At ten years of age, I often got tiny growths on my eyelid called styes. They looked like blisters or tiny pimples along the outer rim of my eyelid. They were red and painful to touch, and a doctor recommended having them removed surgically to prevent them from coming back. *We don't know what we don't know.* No one had explained the process of the surgery to remove the styes.

I remember the whole nightmare experience in detail. I had laid on a flat table covered with a sheet and some nurses held me in a restraining jacket to keep me perfectly still. A nurse or doctor came at me with a long needle aimed at the inside corner of my eye. I screamed, but no one seemed to hear. They were moving in the direction of my face! My mom, facing the outside window, seemed to be having a meltdown. Her tears and emotions were out of control. I didn't know moms could stay right beside their child and provide a soothing voice or touch until I had my own children.

Shock number two: The nurse or doctor came toward me with an apparatus that looked like a muzzle. They placed it over my mouth and nose and told me to breathe. It smelled awful and made me feel sick to my stomach. I woke up still on the table with a patch over my eye. Mom processed the experience as her trauma, rather than mine.

I still felt sick to my stomach while Mom and I had to ride an elevator. I felt groggy, like my legs wouldn't hold me up. It seemed I needed to forget that day because no one talked about it. No one asked if I felt scared or explained why the doctor had to do it. I guess I tucked the memory away somewhere. It got lost. The family I grew up in didn't talk about what hurt them.

Alone in my hospital room one day, I wrote a new song called "Behind a Wall." I suspect my adult personality wrote it for C.J. The soft, gentle tempo told a story about a little girl who had been hurt by someone's sin, while she took the blame. A wall went up around her to keep her safe, but the wall also kept her from receiving the love she needed.

Finishing the song, I wanted to share it with another patient, who I'll call Jack, who I'd grown close to. Jack was a pastor who struggled with manic depression. He listened to my playing, saying almost nothing.

"What?" I quipped defensively.

"Something is missing. I don't know what. It seems like there should be more," Jack said.

I exited Jack's room in a huff, thinking, *Who cares what he thinks! It's my song. If it needed something I would know.*

Anger, my elusive emotion, appeared as I sat on the edge of my bed, guitar in hand, writing the bridge to the song.

I returned to Jack's room knowing the lyrics were complete.

"Behind a Wall"

Words/music: Jeanie Connell. 1986.

There is a child behind a wall, she doesn't see or hear Your voice.

She can't receive somebody's love, she never counts or has a choice.

She's waiting there for someone strong to break the wall and set her free.

She reaches out, nobody's there, no one but me.

She isn't bad, it's not her fault, she lost her way, got locked inside.

Somebody's sins and their deep hurts were all it took, she ran to hide.

And then her God, He built a wall to keep her safe till she could know

About His love, about His grace, He loves her so.

BRIDGE: But though His love is really there, the little girl has got to care!

She has to yell and scream it out! The anger's what it's all about.

Don't let her die! Reach out and try.

It matters not how old or young, we all have hurts, we all have walls.

> *We can pretend they don't exist and yet we all must take our*
> *falls.*
> *If we'll allow ourselves to look and search for God in people's*
> *eyes,*
> *He is the Truth, He crumbles walls, He shatters lies.*

God had some walls to crumble and lies to shatter in my future.

My medical chart was a possession of the doctors. I overheard Dr. Meier look at my chart and confirm a diagnosis: "Patient suffers from depression."

Whirling around, I confronted him defensively, "What me? Depressed? That's what you call a person who can't get out of bed in the morning. That is someone who's always sad. That's not me!"

My doctor responded calmly, knowing I had taken offense at his choice of words. "Jeanie, do you ever feel alone when you are in a room full of people?"

"Well, yes, I do."

Dr. Meier's next question was, "Do you find yourself smiling on the outside when you feel differently inside? Or feel irritated and angry without understanding why?"

Again, I answered yes.

His last question was, "Do you know what it feels like to lose your joy in doing something you used to enjoy?" my psychiatrist inquired.

"Yes, I know that feeling," I answered.

"That's all I indicated on your chart. I didn't mean to upset you," Dr. Meier continued.

"I see from your history that you were previously a patient of Dr. Williams in North Carolina. I learned a great deal from him years ago as a professor of psychology at Duke University."

Hesitantly, I reported the details of my doctor-patient relationship under Dr. Williams' care. "While repeatedly sitting close with him at the end of each appointment, he encouraged me to sit in his lap and the invitation made me uncomfortable," I disclosed. "Our eighteen months ended at that time, and I chose not to continue my therapy with him."

Dr. Meier could have defended his colleague's behavior, but instead he validated my feelings. "I'm so sorry to know that happened. That is not the kind of professional code of conduct I would expect from Dr. Williams. Even if he felt he acted in your best interest, I don't condone his treatment."

Those words from a respected psychiatrist who knew Dr. Williams proved to be healing for me.

Grateful for Dr. Meier and his honesty, I never felt anything but safe with him.

Months later, I passed on to Dr. Williams the remarks that his former medical student shared with me. He offered no apology or regrets. "The method I chose to treat your diagnosis is what I believed you needed," he justified himself. I wondered how many of his patients received the same type of close personal care.

The teaching we received during the hospital's education classes helped us to understand and relate to our issues. Highly trained doctors and authors explained in layman's terms what we could expect as we continued to improve our mental health and how to handle our emotions.

Occupational Therapy was hospital language for arts and crafts, and it included storytelling and other activities. All patients entered the large room with tables and chairs to work individually on our projects—everything from building magazine racks to making key chains and picture frames. Working with our hands seemed to give our minds a rest and made each of us feel good to produce something worthwhile.

When I learned that I had to go home, I was puzzled as to why my doctors, therapists, and entire team of helpers agreed that my time to leave Texas and return home had arrived. It never occurred to me that our insurance had run out. Besides, six weeks away from Michael and our kids was long enough. We were ready to be reunited.

Like my song lyrics mentioned in Chapter 10 from "Always in a Hurry" said, *I could win the race by taking it at a slow pace. No longer in a hurry.*

Chapter 12
ONE STEP AT A TIME

Before I left Texas, Cynthia invited me to write some devotions for a twelve-step book in preparation for the publisher Thomas Nelson. My twelve entries were included in *One Step at a Time*—a title not chosen until after I had written a song by the same title.

Cynthia's devotional with my entries gave the perfect title for this chapter of my life. After I wrote the song "Behind a Wall," which is printed in the middle of the last chapter, it seemed the wall was coming down and C.J. was growing stronger. I could no longer refuse to take notice of her. Our lives were changing. Could my marriage to Michael weather the storm?

Michael's expectations were realistic. His comment, "Jeanie, Texas gave you the tools to move forward," showed wisdom.

We had both changed in the six weeks I'd been away. I found Michael now giving himself permission to set boundaries. When I wanted to talk, he had a choice in the matter. If he was tired after a day at work, he would request a more convenient time. He no longer took on a role to fix me.

Most of our conversations centered on me and my emotions. Cynthia had uncovered the truth; Michael had every reason to be exhausted.

Back home with Kyle and Libby, I wanted to be the mom they needed, but I didn't trust myself to fulfill that role. With C.J. becoming more persistent, my adult persona seemed to grow weaker and less confident.

When I returned to Dr. Ross's office, he said, "I've missed seeing you around here, Jeanie."

"You missed me?" I repeated. Happy to be missed, I had a question for my psychiatrist. "Dr. Ross, I've been thinking about something."

"What's that?" he inquired.

"At first I didn't like having a woman therapist in Texas. After I learned to trust her, she helped me to see things differently," I continued.

Dr. Ross seemed skeptical, "Where are you headed with this?"

"I like being back in your office. I feel safe here. I wondered, since your wife, Jill, is a therapist, if we could work together sometimes. Please don't say no. Just tell me you will think about it," I pleaded.

"I will consult with Jill, and we can talk about it during your next appointment."

The following week Dr. Ross delivered his answer: "Jeanie, Jill and I discussed your idea, and she has agreed to be your therapist. Your weekly appointments will be in her office just down the hall. I will still be available if you need to check in with me."

I knew better than to be overly dramatic, but inside my heart leaped for joy. *Hooray! Hooray! My psychiatrist and therapist live in the same house. How could I possibly have a better team to work with?*

My first sixty minutes in Jill's office were a dream come true. I didn't know if my new therapist knew anything about me. I concluded in our first hour that she had beauty inside and out. She spoke softly and I felt safe. "Jeanie, Dr. Ross and I each have children from previous marriages, but we don't have a child together. You can be the child we never had. Would you like that?" Jill asked.

Timidly, I said yes, while nodding my head up and down. Surely, she recognized C.J., and this had to be the best gift God had ever given me. Only He knew how to satisfy the longing I'd carried for a lifetime.

Fairly certain Jill would tell Dr. Ross of our arrangement, I told no one else. I had a wonderful new secret.

Feeling overjoyed, I ordered balloons and sent them to their office. I called Dr. Ross, asking if he knew what Jill had told me.

"Yes, I think that's one of the wildest things she's ever said," he responded. He never shared his opinion, only his surprised reaction. Believing I'd found the stand-in mom and dad I had searched for, I readily imagined my relationship with them would last forever. I wanted to be whole and healthy. I even wanted to graduate from their care. But C.J. dreaded the day when they might no longer be part of her life.

I could only hope that God would inspire my doctor and therapist to know what I needed, which direction to take, and when I could manage the next step.

It felt safe to share my fears and my tears with Jill. I remember crying in her office only once as she held me in reassurance that neither she nor Dr. Ross were going to leave me. During this season of our relationship, it would have been impossible to imagine I would leave them someday. This stage of psychotherapy called for one step at a time.

Jill was everything I wanted, and everything I didn't, at the same time. C.J. longed to be taken care of like a child, while the adult thirtysomething my family knew as wife and mom had a different perspective. Wanting to be in control, I resented anyone telling me what to do.

Whether Jill realized it or not, she got two patients for the price of one. She had keen instincts, knowing when to encourage my independence and when to acknowledge my need to rely on her.

In the early weeks of our appointments, I began reading a book about someone's trauma and treatment. When I mentioned this to Jill, I confessed the negative reaction I had as I read it. Because it troubled me, Jill suggested I put it down and discontinue reading it. This time was the first of many that I would disregard her to make my own choices, I plunged deeper into the book. As the subject matter now interfered with my sleep and moods, I called Jill, begging for an appointment.

Her first question: "Have you been reading the book we discussed?"

Looking for Jill's sympathy, I replied, "I have, but I didn't know it would continue to be so upsetting! Please can I come and talk with you?"

"We can discuss it at your next regularly scheduled appointment," she said matter-of-factly.

Furious, I called Dr. Ross, hoping he would see it from my perspective. This call was the first of numerous times I tried to get my way by approaching them separately, yet it was always a waste of time. They had a way of bringing my anger to the surface! Much more effective than a quiet room with boxing gloves. When C.J. appealed to Jill and failed to get her way, she attempted to receive a more favorable outcome from Dr. Ross.

My experience has taught me that my greatest level of anger emerges when I am angry with myself. Reading the book against Jill's advice was the act of the child who eats a whole carton of ice cream and is surprised afterward to have a stomachache.

During one of our hourly sessions, I asked Jill if I could be in charge of bringing the sixty minutes to a close. When she agreed, I felt a supreme sense of control. As it came time to leave, I made one request after another, combined with asking non-stop questions, taking advantage of my new responsibility. When Jill announced our time had run out, I couldn't hide my anger. *I just knew she wouldn't keep her promise! That was my job, and she took it.*

I knew from parenting my own children that, when they asked for new responsibilities, they had to learn how to accomplish tasks for themselves. At times, they were unable to complete those tasks and as parents we had to step in. Kids can feel undermined. As a parent I needed to step in. I wanted my children to have time to complete the task I had assigned to them, rather than believe I would take it away if it wasn't done in the way or timeframe I hoped for.

C.J. felt like she failed. Instead of causing Jill to feel proud of her, she lost her new privilege.

In my thirties I had no clue how to handle my anger in a healthy way. I knew how to stuff it away. Hide it. Blame it. I knew the Bible verse, "In your anger do not sin. Do not let the sun go down while you are still angry," Ephesians 4:26 NIV.

What the heck? How did that work?

Because I was frequently asked to bring my guitar and sing with young children during this time period of my life, I felt compelled to write a song about anger. Before I shared the melody with a group of three-and four-year-old's, I asked the question, "What can we do when we have anger inside of us, and how do we let it out?"

One after the other the children offered suggestions. My favorites are: "Through our eyes" and "Through our mouths." Tears and talking seemed like healthy ways to give our anger an outlet.

"One Step at a Time"
Words/music: Jeanie Connell, 1991

One little step at a time
We'll take it one little step at a time.
One little question, one little answer
One little song to rhyme.

One little prayer at a time,
With the patience to wait till we know,
Where God is leading, When do we hear Him?
Which way are we to go?

CHORUS:
And as we go, we stop to see
The tiny bird, a tender tree,
A rainbow up across the sky,
The sound of laughter, or a cry.

One little step at a time
With a message of love in our heart,
Learning to fear Him, Seeking forgiveness,
Setting His love apart.

CHORUS:
How often the Lord is very near
When we are willing to wait and hear.

He speaks through children, have you heard,
The love proclaimed within His Word?
God is there if we'll take the time,
Ready to work when I'm
Trusting in Him just One Little Step at a Time.

Listen to this song on Jeanie's *Roots* CD,
available at jeanieconnell.org.

Chapter 13
REGRETS

We were still in North Carolina and active members of a local church when Michael felt called to be part of the mission team headed for Korea. He would be away about six weeks. I shared his excitement at the opportunity. Friends at the church reached out to Kyle, Libby, and me in his absence.

One night, having dinner with close friends, I developed a migraine headache. (A frequent malady.) I was unable to drive home so our friends invited the three of us to spend the night. Kyle bunked with their son, Libby slept in a bedroom on the main floor, while I slept on the pullout sofa in the basement. They had a lovely home decorated with fashionable furniture and an air of cozy.

They were part of a small group that we met with regularly and were well acquainted with the doctors I had been seeing.

The intense pain of the migraine carried my thoughts to fantasies of someone taking care of me like a dependent child. C.J. imagined Jill and Dr. Ross playing that part. As my physical pain increased, the sense of helplessness became more intense. If I fixated on their remarks during my years in treatment, it became easy to envision them as sympathetic parents, and certainly believable to C.J.

Suddenly, during my delusions, I recognized the cries of Libby, my own little seven-year-old. She sounded scared, and I wanted to go to her. I alone could comfort her and soothe her fears. But lying on the pullout sofa in my own world, focused on C.J.'s needs, I pretended not to hear. Unable to erase the memory of putting my needs ahead of Libby's, I would someday need to let go of the guilt and forgive myself.

By God's grace, my friend, who had been awakened by Libby's cries, brought her downstairs. I felt so thankful to have her beside me. I still remember my emotional pain that night, loving my precious daughter and trying to comfort C.J. with nothing more than delusions. Being a mother. Needing a mother. This event would never become a topic for therapy.

Why? My shame. My fears. I didn't want to admit my fantasies to the professionals who worked with me. I didn't want to let them go. *What would they think of me?* I valued my relationship with them at all costs. On occasion, when I reached out to Jill, she would return my call and Libby would answer the phone. Jill would identify herself and say, "Please tell your mom that I called. She may have just needed to hear my voice."

"Hear her voice!" Libby would wail. "You do not need to hear Jill's voice, Mom! I hate it when she says things like that! Please don't go back to see her! You don't need her! You always feel worse when you come home from an appointment!" my only daughter exclaimed.

Out of the mouths of babes…

I had no way to communicate to my daughter that I had a personality living inside my mind and heart who believed she needed what Jill and Dr. Ross imparted.

The words out of Libby's mouth showed her awareness of my growing dependence—unhealthy dependence—that I remained unwilling to recognize. I continued to view C.J. as separate from me. As I look back on my years with Jill and Dr. Ross, I'm sure they saw us as one and the same. *Or did they?*

C.J. was a people pleaser and felt cared for when Jill gave her rules to follow. My adult personality followed a different set of rules: her own. One of my rules was going to every event I could. So, when I heard about a retreat not far from home in Charlotte, North Carolina, I went. I met a therapist there whose practice captured my curiosity. Tempted to schedule a visit, I mentioned it to Jill, who strongly advised against it. "Jeanie, I think you have enough to handle coming to see me each week. The last thing you need is an additional therapist."

I chose to ignore Jill's advice and make my own decision. I made an appointment and drove down the expressway feeling grown up and confident.

The check-in process in this counselor's office had the usual amount of paperwork. I was invited to join some sort of group session with about twenty other patients who gathered in a large room. Knowing no one and finding a seat on the carpeted floor, like the others, I had my back to the wall. Watching the drama unfold like a movie in a theater, I had no intention of being in the cast of characters.

One by one, each patient came forward when called, to lie on the ground and be wrapped in a large white bedsheet. I felt more and more nervous at what I saw, and I was planning to escape.

As each patient was wrapped up, he or she resembled a mummy and were encouraged to scream out at anything or anyone they were angry with. Those of us sitting around the room, either with legs crossed or straight out in front of us, looked on. Scared to death that my name would be next, I knew that I wanted no part of this exercise or this type of therapy.

Dang! Why did Jill have to be right again? I should have never come. Why didn't I take her advice?

Quietly I slipped away from the room, fortunate to avoid the remainder of the experience.

I wanted to learn from my mistakes, but it seemed I kept repeating them.

Months later, before I arrived at my scheduled appointment with Jill, I intentionally took too many of my prescription pills for migraines. Like the overdose in my first year with Dr. Ross, this time I finished off more than half the bottle. Since I didn't show signs of an overdose when I arrived in Jill's office, she treated me with kindness, bringing me crackers from the vending machine. My plan wasn't to end my life. I was once again seeking to be nurtured and taken care of like a child. The pills also kept me from accepting and dealing with my depression and anxiety for the moment.

I dreaded owning up to the truth, but as an hour slipped away, I knew I had to confess what I had done.

Apparently, Dr. Ross was out of the office with a "tummy bug" (as Jill called it), so she took matters into her own capable hands. She led me to another office where I slept on the sofa. No conversation took place between us. I didn't black out, but with a nurse frequently checking my blood pressure and vital signs, I knew having my stomach pumped was an option. My repeated attempts for attention were only making matters worse, and I felt like a huge failure.

No matter how others were being affected by my behavior, I was in my safe place where I met with Jill and Dr. Ross.

I knew the staff members were trying to reach Michael, and believe it or not, I had given no thought as to how he would play into the scenario.

I heard Dr. Ross's voice in the hallway, but I never saw or spoke to him. I wondered why he had come into the office.

I gave no thought to inconveniencing him, Jill, or, for that matter, my husband. Once again, C.J. existed in her own world.

By God's grace, I escaped having my stomach pumped. Michael had been reached and was waiting in the car for me. My belongings were returned to me and, rather than show any type of gratitude to anyone, I reached in my purse and took *more* pills from the prescription bottle. Finally, I witnessed Michael's anger and bewilderment. "Jeanie, what's going on?"

he asked. "What are you thinking?" His words were few, but his tone of voice spoke volumes.

I loathed myself and hated my actions.

I didn't know what I wanted other than love and attention.

How could anyone love me when I couldn't accept myself?

"Growing Up"
Words/music: Jeanie Connell, 1986

CHORUS: What do ya say I grow up?
What do ya say I let go?
I never liked the word maturity,
So, I just don't know.
But God's word is clear,
He's calling me to know,
He wants me off the milk and onto food,
Building me up, so that I can grow.

ENDING CHORUS: Building me up, reaching a faith,
Speaking the Truth,
So, into Christ I'll grow.

It sounds scary to me
Just to be set free.
I thought I wanted someone's loving arms
Always around me.
My thinking needs to be
No more the childish kind.
I want to be secure in Christ and put childish ways behind.

ENDING CHORUS

Chapter 14
ONLY ONCE

During my next session with Dr. Ross, I became aware of the anger I provoked in Jill, himself, and Michael. I needed their forgiveness as well as my own.

I remember my follow-up meeting with Jill. I asked if she would witness me disposing of the remaining pills from my prescription for migraine headaches. She followed me across the hall to the restroom as I flushed the pills. Not only did I never take them again but I also never needed them again. At least one of the symptoms that brought me to counseling had been eradicated. Any breakthrough seemed slow. Unaware, this gradual process prepared me to become acquainted with the Healer.

Ambivalence was always part of my relationship with Jill. I would push her away, yet I wanted her close.

"I don't feel good today," I announced softly as our sacred hour began.

"I'm sorry to hear that, Jeanie. Do you still want to stay and talk with me?" Jill asked.

Being in the same room with Jill or Dr. Ross always seemed worth the $100 price tag.

At the end of our session, she placed her hand on my forehead to see if I had a fever. I had no memory of anyone ever doing that. The feeling of being loved and cared for inspired the song at the end of this chapter. The moment became a memory.

I knew little about my therapist. She had a son and a daughter; I didn't know their names.

"Tell me a true story," C.J. would plead.

Jill would oblige. "After my son went away to camp, he came home and told me he had a wonderful time, and he didn't even miss me."

Poor Jill. Didn't she want her son to miss her?

Then the conversation got interesting. "Someday, Jeanie, when you no longer see me and Dr. Ross, you will have us in your head."

"I don't want you in my head!" I blurted out. "I want to see you and touch you!" (How does one explain the concept of loss, separation, or death to a child for the first time? No one will be around forever.)

I loved hearing bits and pieces of Jill's life as a mom. They told her story.

As she sat beside her desk, C.J. moved to the floor next to her. "Can I put my head right here?" pointing to her lap.

"Yes, but it's almost time to leave for today," her soothing voice reminded me. The words. The short-lived moments, over the years, became strung together like lights on a Christmas tree. They became my smiling memories.

When Dr. Ross and Jill took a vacation, C.J. felt miserable. Abandoned. Jill would make me feel better by telling me, "It's okay to wish." I loved those words.

Dr. Ross and Jill always returned as promised. In the seven years I scheduled appointments with them, they were always faithful and showed up when they said they would. They were consistent. I could count on their words to be true.

One day, several weeks later, therapy connected to something that happened in my childhood. As I've mentioned, I only had a handful of childhood memories, so those few were significant. My younger sister, Kathy, and I loved dolls. Baby dolls. Big dolls. Small dolls. But always *new* dolls. The smell of a new doll, nothing short of intoxicating, connects to my sweetest memory.

My sisters and I were young, maybe twelve, ten, and five, when our parents bought all three of us a brand-new, life-size doll. Standing three feet tall in their colorful outfits and matching shoes, they were posed in front of our Christmas tree. The blonde for Kathy, the brunette for my older sister, Barbie, and the redhead for me.

We were all so excited to retrieve our own look-alike doll! Although I never shared my favorite memory with any of my doctors or counselors, C.J. had shared the desire to have a doll with Jill since she'd given me permission to make a wish.

Settled on the cozy sofa several weeks later, Jill announced,

"Jeanie, I brought you something," and handed me a used doll.

C.J. didn't want to hurt her feelings, but she couldn't hold the doll against her face and breathe in the smell of a *new* doll. She thanked Jill while hiding her true feelings.

As children, we often can't express gratitude for something because "it" wasn't what we actually wanted. Kids are disappointed not to find the *one* thing they were looking for. Adults can be at a loss because they can't figure out what "it" is or how it can be attained. Substitutes are worthless to a kid.

As adults, we try to find substitutes for things that we want or need all the time, but the replacements are still not quite the same. We even try to substitute God in our life with other things to fill the void, but nothing can serve as a substitute for Him.

Looking back now, I can recognize what I really wanted: to be someone's special little girl—worthy of a brand-new doll. My wish tapped into one of the rare memories I had.

Jill and I never discussed where the doll she gave me came from. It was possibly a hand-me-down or picked up from the Goodwill.

The small used doll sat on the shelf behind our waterbed at home, threatening to expose C.J. Michael never mentioned the doll, and with ambivalent emotions, I decided to throw her away without telling my therapist.

When Libby turned five, I made her a life-size doll, with yarn for hair and a floppy cotton body. It stood taller than our Christmas dolls. At age ten, Libby had no further interest in the homemade rag doll, so I decided to bring her to Jill's office in hopes she would be reminded of me throughout the week.

C.J. imagined the large doll sitting propped up on the cozy sofa. (C.J. was always on a quest to be special.) Sadly, the results that awaited me left me feeling anything but special.

Before my next appointment with Jill, I realized that my doll had gone missing. We didn't talk about it. My worry bordered on obsession as I wondered what had become of my large rag doll. Rather than ask Jill, I inquired of Dr. Ross, questioning if he had noticed it anywhere.

"I remember seeing the big doll, Jeanie, but I have never seen her at our house. I will look into it for you," he said.

Dr. Ross reported back saying, "Jill had to fold up your doll and stuff it into a cabinet in her office because another patient felt uncomfortable. The doll scared her."

Scared her?! Stuffed in a cabinet?! Clearly, another patient had priority over me. My plan completely backfired. If Jill could toss away my doll, I concluded she wanted no reminders of me. When the doll wasn't on display at the office, it was hurtful to me. Maybe an explanation from Jill could have softened the blow.

Taking a small, pink, soft doll that hung out with some teddy bears, C.J. put her in a box and mailed it to my psychiatrist and therapist. But first she cut it in half. (*Ouch, that had to hurt!*) I wanted to show them that I didn't care about a dumb old doll anyway. In truth, I did. I cared.

It never occurred to me that kids break toys to get attention. C.J. seemed so separate from me in her actions, with a distinctly different mindset.

Jewel, another therapist at the same clinic, worked primarily with kids. They called it play therapy. Jill signed me up. I didn't have to talk when I spent time with Jewel unless I wanted to. I had permission to work with her every other week, which meant not seeing Jill as often.

My first appointment with Jewel felt safe. Handing me a lump of clay, she said, "Jeanie, you can make anything you would like."

I created a miniature birthday cake about two inches wide by two inches high. It had clay candles on it that I stuck into the cake. I had no memories of any childhood birthday parties. Unconsciously, I made the cake for C.J. I had no intentions of giving away my tiny sculpture. It seemed an innocent expression of the past I was unable to remember.

During my second session with Jewel, she gave me a very large sheet of paper that covered the entire table in front of me. We marked a timeline on it, from before my birth until the present day. I could draw pictures of any event in my whole life, even things I couldn't remember. I drew a picture marking my sister Kathy's birth. I made a mark where my grampa died. I didn't like the timeline as much as I liked the birthday cake. My school years and marriage were noted too.

Jewel had three rules:

  1) Don't hurt yourself.

2) Don't hurt other people.

3) Don't hurt anyone's stuff.

Jill left a large phone book on the shelf in Jewel's office for me. If I ever felt really angry, I could tear it to pieces. *What a silly idea. I am sure I will never need to rip up a phone book.*

I respected Jewel's rules.

During the next session of play therapy, I felt angry and wanted to see my psychiatrist. I knew that Jewel had communicated my request to Dr. Ross. *Why would he say no?*

Jewel led me down the hall to Jill's empty office to wait, and I grabbed the phone book on my way out. I sat there on the cozy sofa in Jill's office all by myself and waited. And waited. And waited.

The longer I waited, the angrier C.J. became. Having nothing better to do, I picked up the large, heavy phone book and ripped it to pieces. My anger escalated when I discovered the pages could only be ripped if I tore out a few pages at a time. Arghhh!

The more C.J. tugged at the pages, the more irritated she became. Like adding fuel to a fire, her anger increased.

That Dr. Ross kept me waiting only caused my frustration to climb. *Would he ever come check on me? Didn't he care? Where could he be? Could someone else be more important than me?*

Unconcerned that Jill's office was now filling with torn pieces of paper, I could feel my anger still growing like the stacks of ripped pages on the carpet. It occurred to me that this exercise could prove much more effective than going to the quiet room in Texas.

Finally! Dr. Ross came through the door, trying hard not to laugh. He said, "What a magnificent mess, Jeanie! You have done a remarkable job of expressing anger."

My aggravation dissolved like an ice cube on hot cement. "I have?" I questioned.

My doctor continued, "You've done some important work here today and displayed quite some temper tantrum."

I thought temper tantrums were for little kids who didn't get their way.

Dr. Ross left the office in search of something to hold the rubble spread over the floor. He returned with the largest, industrial-strength, black trash bag either of us had ever seen.

With both of us laughing at the size of the plastic bag, he exited again, instructing me to clean up my mess. His reappearance earned me another compliment: "Good job, Jeanie."

As I moved toward him to receive my customary hug, he stepped back. "Whoa! Look at your hands, they are covered in black from the newsprint. No goodbye hug today."

A few days later, Michael and I received a request from my psychiatrist's office to meet with him, Jill, and Jewel. I felt nervous, like being called to the principal's office in school. Michael and C.J. were not acquainted. Just having him in the room would feel awkward.

The three professionals working with me had called the

meeting to determine the best course of treatment for me.

Michael and I sat on the cozy sofa together, although I would rather have been on the floor, close to Dr. Ross. I kept my head down during the consultation, choosing not to speak. Everyone had an opportunity to share their thoughts. Michael spoke up, "I know Jeanie misses seeing Jill when she has an appointment with Jewel."

Dr. Ross followed his remark: "Jill and I feel that play therapy is getting her too stirred up."

Stirred up sounds like chocolate milk, and I don't understand how that could be a bad thing.

I remained quiet along with Jewel. Jill addressed the next question to me: "Jeanie, would you like us to make the decision for you?"

Nodding my head up and down conveyed my agreement. I felt protected and cared for as they made the decision to terminate my appointments with Jewel.

Speaking for the first time: "I like Jewel."

As usual, Jill had her take-charge response: "The decision has been made, and we will stay with that." Decisive. Confident. I liked that, except when I didn't.

Dr. Ross looked at me as though he thought the gathering had left me exhausted or helpless. "Jeanie, we can revisit the decision later if we need to." He touched me on the head as he left the office.

As much as I wanted Jill to make my decisions, something inside me resisted when she did. We had stormy times ahead...more like a hurricane than a thunderstorm.

Hearing the following song, audiences have asked me if I wrote it for my mother. I tell them, "No, it's about my therapist—and Jesus."

"Only Once"
Words/music: Jeanie Connell

Only once she spoke the words I longed to hear her say,
Only once she held me when I cried,
Only once her hand reached out in such a gentle way,
And yet it never seemed like only once.
Because a hundred times or more I lived it over in my mind,
I think a hundred times or more it made me smile.
I guess a hundred times or more it was a memory I could find,
So it just never seemed like only once.
Only once He hung upon a cross in agony,
Only once they nailed His hands and feet,
Only once He suffered every sin for you and me,
And yet it never seemed like only once.
Because a hundred times or more I heard the story told again,
I think a hundred times or more it made me cry;
*To think that once so long ago, **one life** could change the lives of men,*
Well, it just never seemed like only once.

BRIDGE: In life the best and the worst are the moments we recall,
And yet most of our life is in between.
May we try to reach out with the greatest love of all,
And may it never seem like only once. May our love never seem like only once.

Chapter 15
MOM

Mike's mom, Mom Connell, had only boys, so when she got daughters-in-law, she treated us better than our own moms. She enjoyed buying us girlie gifts, going to her favorite restaurants, and introducing us to her friends at her women's events.

However, she did not understand my eating disorder or the years I spent in therapy, not to mention the hospitalizations. I felt guilty and greatly lacking in my role as a mom. Our dialog about these treatments were nonexistent. I am not sure what she thought. Her generation believed, "If you can't say something nice, don't say anything at all." Clearly, she did not have anything helpful or encouraging to say where my illness was concerned.

For several years, I would sing and share my story at mother-daughter banquets. It was a good gig, although Libby wanted nothing to do with it. She knew the attention would not be on her, but on the women who gathered. It provided the perfect venue for my songs.

"Mother-in-Law"
Words/music: Jeanie Connell

Well, I'm gonna sing a song about a mother-in-law,
She's not exactly like a mother, you know.
We got related through a marriage to her charming son
About (twenty) years ago.
And though she never interferes with how I'm running my house
Or what I'm cooking for my family,
I think there's times when she wonders if her son will be healthy
Eating just my recipes.
Well, just imagine living only with your family tree
And then suddenly one day
You've got a daughter who is coming from a different mold,
A mold she thought they'd thrown away.
Although my chicken's not as crisp, nor my chili as hot,
She seems to take it all in her stride.
And when we have a disagreement between husband and wife,
I'm really touched when she takes my side.
She never says, "I told you so," or "Won't you do it my way?"
But when we need her, she always comes through.
There's no one else in the world that I really could say
I'd like to be related to. I love you, Mom!

My relationship with Michael's parents began when I started to fall in love with their son.

Although I had a choice when I chose Michael and his family, we don't get to choose our biological families. It can be challenging to overlook weaknesses and praise each other's strengths. Being related, however, means that my sorrows have an impact on my family.

I had reached the point in therapy when they emphasized the strong need for a face-to-face confrontation about difficult issues. I did not look forward to it.

Still lacking Kodak moments, I would begin the confrontation with the fact that Mom's father, a pedophile, had molested both Kathy and our mom according to their own admissions.

Michael and I met with my parents at a neutral location, an equal distance from both of us. We got a hotel room. Mom and Dad did the same. After dinner, we met back in my parents' room to talk.

I gently and truthfully reviewed the facts concerning Grampa. Mom's view of right and wrong had been skewed by her father's actions, and she had never confronted those lies with the truth. Although she knew what happened to Kathy as a child and admitted her own experience, she seemed incapable of connecting the dots. Mom could not accept the fact that her dad had inflicted damage on her daughters by his perverted behavior. Her loyalty as a daughter overshadowed his criminal behavior. Sadly, she needed to defend her dad rather than recognize the injury he had inflicted on her as his only daughter.

I recalled Jill's words to me, "Jeanie, your mom may never change. That will be her choice. But that doesn't mean that *you* can't change." I was and am grateful for those words. In the meeting with my parents, I never brought up my flashbacks or the fragmented parts of my life. Instead, I focused on the facts that had already come to light. I hoped my parents could be sympathetic to the years I had spent in therapy seeking help. They, however, did not support my treatment in psychotherapy. It had never been something they had experienced. Surely God's love, along with prayers, would suffice to put my past behind me once and for all. But putting our past behind us comes after we have faced the truth and the consequences.

I wanted their unconditional love, with them knowing the hurts and issues I had been dealing with. I loved my parents. I didn't doubt their love for me. When I brought up my grandfather's sexual abuse of Kathy, Mom, and Mom's girlfriends, I was surprised by her extreme reaction. She had a complete meltdown in the corner of their hotel room, hurling accusations as though my words had been chosen to attack her. Her threatening look displayed aggressive anger, like a weapon. Intense emotions mixed with burning tears left Mom unable to handle any form of communication. I didn't judge her. I felt sad that neither of my parents were able to show me the tenderness and compassion I needed. I don't think they understood the impact Grampa's sins had on our entire family.

My dad had an expression on his face that conveyed deep disappointment and defeat. It seemed all the unwanted emotions in the room were my fault. Having a story that I needed to tell caused me to report something no one wanted to hear. I wanted to put the confrontation behind me.

Michael spoke up, "Babe, we need to leave now." He was and is like a blanket of love and protection at times.

I knew we had accomplished something unpleasant that needed to be done. I had to remind myself that confronting may not always bring the outcome we imagine. A confrontation is like seeing a dentist—I will be the one to benefit and the one to feel the relief from the pain. I felt comforted from Reinhold Niebuhr's prayer (1951): "Lord, grant me the serenity to accept the things I cannot change, courage to change the things I can, and wisdom to know the difference."

My mom had no say over the way her father behaved. We don't choose our parents, nor do we choose the choices they make. I can only imagine the pain my mom felt in exposing her own daughters to the sins of her father.

Jill helped me to understand that denying that pain became my mom's way of coping.

I will close with a song I wrote for my mom. She loved listening to Kathy and me sing together. We would share familiar hymns, lullabies, old camp songs, or original melodies. Our voices—sisters' voices—blended with a unique harmony.

"Mom"

Words/music: Jeanie Connell

Who says, "You're gorgeous," when your mirror tells you yuck?
Who says, "You're thin," although your zipper's getting stuck?
Who's there to bail you out when you're down on your luck?
Could only be Mom, just your mom.

Who gives you confidence when you don't have a date?
Who can still convince you that you're absolutely great?
Who makes you think you'd be the world's most perfect mate?
Could only be Mom, just your mom.

Who thinks you're best of all when you know you're the worst?
Who shares your joy when you're so happy you could burst?
Who makes fourth place look good when you just wanted first?
Could only be Mom, just your mom.

Who's there to hold your hand when no one else will do?
Who sees you at your worst but still loves you for you?
Who taught you prayers, drove you to school, baked cookies too?
Could only be Mom, just your mom.
There's only one mom...just your mom.

Chapter 16
AN UNEXPECTED SURPRISE

Michael and I were unprepared for the surprise God planned to give us. With a son almost fourteen, a daughter almost nine, and myself on the verge of forty, I became pregnant. With child.

I have never claimed to have the gift of prophecy, but this unplanned pregnancy came with an unexpected word about our future. Before a baby began to grow in my womb, I heard the Lord tell me that we were going to have a son and he would be born on March 12 the following year. I waited before telling Michael. His priceless response: "Jeanie, you missed God."

"I did? How do you know?" I asked.

Michael's calm, commonsense response: "Do you want another child?"

"Well, not really. I'm happy with the two we have."

"So am I!" he agreed happily. "So, you see, what you heard couldn't be God." End of subject.

Eventually, in the months ahead, after I skipped my monthly cycle and took a positive drugstore test, Michael asked me to have our doctor order "real lab work."

After getting over the shock, and I do mean shock, of preparing for another baby, both Michael and I welcomed the gift God wanted to give us.

This experience proved to be the best example up to that point of us trusting God with our future. It was and is not based on what I think or what I want. Father knows best. God's plans have often collided with mine.

At my scheduled appointment with Jill in July 1988, as I took my seat on her cozy sofa, I announced, "I'm pregnant. The baby is due in March."

"Wow, I didn't see that coming," Jill responded. "How are you feeling, Jeanie?"

"I'm feeling sick almost every day. I'm shocked…and I'm happy. Very. Very happy!" I concluded.

Jill passed on my condition to Dr. Ross, resulting in one of the few times my psychiatrist made absolutely no sense to me.

"Jill told me your news. Well, I guess you really *are* a grown-up now!"

What does my pregnancy have to do with C.J.? Does my doctor think she vanished because I'm carrying a new life inside of me? No sense. No sense at all.

Jill and I managed to have a few adult conversations. She helped me get a grip on the changes in my life. I had lots of questions and I trusted her answers. My therapist seemed so confident. I knew she liked being a mom. I also knew that she couldn't be my mom. I could no longer pretend.

I remember wishing my mom could have the same kind of confidence as Jill. I wanted my mom to love and accept herself.

Michael Kristofer Connell entered the world on March 19, 1989. His due date, March 12, fulfilled the word I received before he was conceived. He brought light into my world. He brought joy to our family, our extended family, and our friends. We named him after Michael and Dr. Chris Thurman from the hospital in Texas.

My world seemed built on healing from a past I couldn't remember. As I loved, sang over, and played with Kris, healing took place inside my heart and soul. This gift of life, breathing life into me, helped me to love the child inside of myself. No doubt he provided all of us with a new beginning.

He looked so identical to his big brother that friends stood amazed. "He looks just like Kyle!" We would respond, "We know." Some continued to stare and repeated it again.

Kris's six-foot-tall brother and nine-year-old sister spent oodles of time with him. Libby would say, "Mom, Kris is going to grow up thinking I am his mother."

"I will take that chance," I would respond, never realizing how close to the truth that would become.

Carrying my baby in his car seat, I transported Kris to my psychiatrist's office, without appointment, to show him off.

Kris continues to be a blessing. He still reminds us of what's important in life. We are all so grateful he completed our family. Giving birth to our son would help me to face the future with hope.

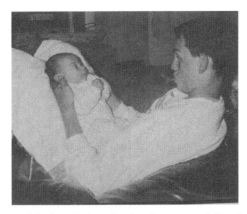

Kyle, 14, and baby Kristofer in Spencer, North Carolina

"Kristofer"
Words/music: Jeanie Connell, March 1989

K-R-I-S-T-O-F-E-R, he's the one who makes us smile.
K-R-I-S-T-O-F-E-R, soft and snuggly, that's his style.

Busy looking, busy moving, watching everyone go past,
Though he sits there, going nowhere, he is running hard and fast.

He's a blessing. Unexpected. He reminds me every day.
Work's important, life is short, and don't forget: Make time to play.

K-R-I-S-T-O-F-E-R, he's the one who makes us smile.
K-R-I-S-T-O-F-E-R, soft and snuggly, that's his style.
We love you, Kris!

Chapter 17
ONCE UPON A TIME

I had mixed feelings about my separate personalities. Could C.J. possibly be merging with me? I wanted to relate to my therapist as an adult but wanted to be sure she would not forget about the little girl.

During my sessions with Jill, I seemed to be spending more time as an adult, a wife, and a mother.

This left C.J. somewhat fearful that Jill could forget her. Feeling split between personalities caused me to wonder how Dr. Ross and Jill were perceiving me. Maybe they didn't want me to grow up. Or maybe they considered my independence a good thing. Either way, I wasn't ready to let go. I needed them and wanted to make that clear. Therefore, I wrote the following letter:

July 11, 1989

To Jill,

I'm glad I got to see you today. I like that you know I am separate from adult Jeanie. At times it seems like you want me to act more like her. Thanks for allowing me to have scared and angry feelings.

I feel jealous of your other patients, especially my friend who I referred to you. How do I make jealous feelings go away?

I'm not happy about your vacation in August, I never know where you are.

By the way, I know you aren't my mom, but sometimes it feels like you are, and it's a nice feeling.

Bye. I love you,

Jeanie (C.J.)

I heard Jill planned to start a support group for women. Being her patient, I assumed I would be invited to attend. When I mentioned it to Jill, she said, "Jeanie, I don't think this is a good time for you to be part of this group." This was said in a tone that indicated she would make the final decision about my inclusion.

Anger became my primary emotion. Furious, I felt I deserved at least some kind of explanation. I had only one recourse—to present my case to Dr. Ross.

Having moved to an office across town, he seemed unaware of Jill's decision. We had some discussion about why I deserved to be part of the support group, but he wouldn't express his views until he had a chance to discuss the matter with his wife.

Anger trumped my feelings of rejection, and I felt offended

to learn that Jill thought I needed time alone with her rather than time in a group setting. My days of wanting her to make my decisions seemed to be slipping away.

After writing and sending her a seventeen-page letter detailing all the reasons I didn't trust her, I got an infuriating response saying she didn't trust me either.

I didn't care about her trust! I was the one who was paying for this relationship!

Several months later Jill paid me the supreme compliment of inviting me into a new support group she would be leading. I graciously accepted, showing great maturity.

After one group session I landed in Dr. Ross's office. "You seem upset, Jeanie. Isn't this the day you were going to attend group therapy?" he inquired.

"I don't want to go back, Dr. Ross," I said, visibly upset and looking for sympathy.

"Oh my, what happened?" he responded, trying to get to the bottom of my impromptu visit. "Did you get into trouble today?" he questioned.

"No," C.J. answered meekly. "I was good."

Dr. Ross smiled while repeating the information, "Oh, you were a good girl today."

"Yes. And Jill paid me no attention!" Words spoken in hopes of gaining my doctor's support.

"Well, I'm sure Jill must have given you some attention."

"Jill is mean, Dr. Ross." I spoke with control.

"Is she mean to all of her patients?" he countered.

That's a strange question.

"No. She is only mean to me!" I continued.

"Is it possible that Jill, determined correctly, a few months ago when she decided you were not quite ready to join a support group?" he inquired gently.

Shrugging my shoulders, C.J. had nothing more to say.

She probably invited me to this group to prove herself right all along. Mean. Just mean.

A few months before my psychiatrist moved his office to a new location, C.J. entered and plunked down on the cozy sofa. "Dr. Ross, would you read me a story?" she asked timidly.

"What kind of a story?" he responded.

"It's a story I wrote called *Little Princess*."

"Jeanie, you are able to read for yourself," Dr. Ross said.

Losing confidence, I inquired, "Don't you ever want someone to read to you?"

"No. I can read for myself," he said matter-of-factly.

I grew quiet, lowering my head, when unexpectedly:

"Once upon a time," my psychiatrist began to read, "there lived a little princess, loved by the king and queen."

I sat spellbound, listening to every word as though I'd never heard it.

At the close of the story Dr. Ross read, "They all ate their biskits and jam?" He chuckled, asking, "Is that supposed to be *biscuits*?"

I felt a little embarrassed that I had misspelled a word as he continued, "Whatever else it is, it is well written."

Memories like this one would play over in my mind through the years, the same way we enjoy our favorite songs.

Whether my appointment was with Dr. Ross or Jill, I secretly hoped they would talk about me afterward. Discuss something I'd said or done, or the progress I'd made. My life revolved around them, so it seemed possible to believe that part of their lives revolved around me.

Jill made it clear that I should not expect them to discuss me outside of their office. This didn't seem possible.

"Don't you like talking to Dr. Ross?" I questioned.

Frustrated, she would reply, "My point, Jeanie, is that I don't want you to expect that to happen."

Jill's words went in one ear and straight out the other as I told myself that she and Dr. Ross cared about me. During my first appointment with Jill, she invited my dependence. *What parents don't want to talk to each other about their child? Why would Jill now discourage that?*

I reminded Jill, "You said I could be the child that you and Dr. Ross never had."

"Isn't it enough that we take care of you?" The words were gently spoken.

Downcast, I responded, "No. It isn't enough."

"Jeanie, I regret telling you that you could be our child."

I had to think long and hard about that comment. Why did Jill ever say it? Did she lie to me? Did she offer it so I could trust her?

This bad news followed good news: her announcement that she would soon be moving her office across town to where Dr. Ross worked.

I could not hide my pleasure, as my feet came right up off the floor!

"Jeanie, keep your feet on the floor. This decision has nothing to do with our seeing you as a patient," she said sternly.

Coming to grips with the professional relationship Jill and Dr. Ross offered rather than them agreeing to serve as the surrogate parents I hoped for left me stumped.

Thankfully, Jesus had a plan in place down to the smallest detail. With perfect timing, He planned my rescue before I knew what I needed. He gave me a song, and four months later, I wrote the following letters to Jill and Dr. Ross.

September 4, 1990

Dear Jill,

Never can I remember wanting so badly to be understood by another as I wanted to be understood by you. Our Sunday school lesson from 2 Timothy 2:15, "Do your best to present yourself to God as one approved. A workman who does not need to be ashamed and who correctly handles the word of truth."

I have approval from people other than God and it brings me no satisfaction. It's time to let go. You gave me permission to leave you. You told me it would happen someday. I would like September 26th to be my graduation day! (I guess I had a plan after all.) I want you to be happy for me and if you agree, I would like to end our sixty-minute session if I promise not to go past time. Also, could you give me a token of some kind to commemorate my "graduation"? The smallest gift would be a reminder for me.

Jeanie

September 1990

Dear Dr. Ross,

It's time for me to let go.

There are a lot of paradoxes in the Christian life. When we're weak, we are strong. If we're willing to lose our life, we will find it. Feeling healed, I recognize a total dependence on God. I can't get through a day without Him. I know I'm pleasing to Him (and you are too). I've tried to elicit love and care from you and Jill like you have for your own children. That is unfair and unrealistic. Only Jesus can give me the safety and security I have longed for.

I love you, but Somebody loves you more,

Jeanie

"Once upon a Time"

Words/music: Jeanie Connell, May 28, 1990

Once upon a time I liked to hear a story,
Once upon a time I wanted only you,
Once upon a time the safest place was your place,
But that was once upon a time and then I grew.
Once upon a time I knew not how to love me,
Once, no more than that, you taught me how.
Once upon a time you held my life together.
Sometimes it's sad that once-upon-a-time could not be now.
I searched night and day; God alone knew what I needed.
Jesus showed the way as my Father interceded.
Once upon a time we hold a hand that's faithful,
Then there comes a time in growing when we know
We can take the hand of Jesus Christ to save us,
There never comes a time when we must let it go.

Once upon a time I miss hearing a story,
Once upon a time I'm missing only you,
Once upon a time the safest place was your place,
But that was once upon a time and then I grew.
Yes, that was once upon a time…and then I grew.

Listen to this song at jeanieconnell.org/music.

Chapter 18
TIME TO SAY GOODBYE

I wrote "Time to Say Goodbye" in 1988 and took my guitar to Dr. Ross's office. I had never shared a song during counseling. My psychiatrist listened intently, and I made a smiling memory. It seems my efforts to say goodbye were a bit premature considering I remained in treatment another four years. Once again, my plans collided with God's.

But writing the song started a disengagement process. At times C.J. felt more like a teen than a toddler. Sharing the song with Dr. Ross felt like moving in the right direction.

Lacking childhood memories, I found counseling to be the best place to deal with my dilemma. I didn't share with others the life I lived behind the closed door of therapy. That chapter of my life remained private and closed.

Which brings me to the reason why I am writing my story as an open book. I believe there are others who wrestle with the guilt, shame, and confusion that take place between them and the person being paid to listen.

Just as the roots of a tree are underground and remain hidden, so are the deeper issues that come from our roots. The only tree without roots is an artificial tree. Likewise, the only people without roots are artificial people, those who are afraid to reveal what is under the surface.

We all know how to look good on the outside. Roots are not the pretty part of a tree, yet they provide the rich growth and beauty from the ground up. God receives glory from the nature revealed in trees and mountains. I pray He will receive glory for the roots and human nature I am led to disclose.

Most of what God has revealed to me, as I've searched for memories, are songs. Music to expose my heart, my longings, and my vulnerable places. He is a good God. The good Shepherd. We can trust Him to care for us as we wander like sheep, get turned upside down, and need help getting back up.

The writer Oliver Goldsmith said, "Success consists of getting up just one more time than you fall."

Jesus never gets weary of helping us up one more time.

A tug-of-war inside me kept me longing to remain in Jill and my doctor's care, even while I also wanted to declare my independence. Just as I began weaning myself off therapy, another doctor became involved.

When I developed an annoying rash during pregnancy, our family doctor, Dr. Evergreen (pseudonym), couldn't give me anything that might affect the baby. But once I gave birth to Kris, he prescribed Prednisone to put an end to the rash.

The tiny pack of pills had me increase the number I took each day before I was supposed to eventually taper them off. Somewhere in the middle of taking this medication, I became unable to sleep. Unable. Sleep would not come. Me being wide awake day and night put a very worried look on my husband's face. I also had an amazing amount of energy. I would clean the whole house late at night and write songs day after day. The most unusual side effect was a paranoia that convinced me each day that death would come. I didn't want to die, but I needed to be prepared to die. I had no intention of harming myself in any way, yet I gave constant warnings that my life would abruptly come to an end. I prepared Michael to expect me to die. I left notes to our kids telling them how much they meant to me, although I never mentioned my premonitions of death.

Michael finally insisted that I call Dr. Evergreen, who had prescribed the medication.

"George, this is Jeanie Connell. I am having an extreme reaction to the Prednisone you prescribed for the rash. I never sleep, and I believe I am going to die. Each day it's a different scenario."

"Jeanie, that reaction is definitely not from the drug, and you cannot stop taking it," my doctor responded. "The entire packet needs to be taken just as prescribed. Now, I must ask you a question: Does anyone in your family suffer from manic depression? I believe that is what you are dealing with."

Exploding with anger: "No! That is ridiculous, Dr. Evergreen. It is this drug!"

Still sounding very sure of himself, he said, "Jeanie, you need to see a psychiatrist and tell them what's happening."

"Fine! A psychiatrist? That's no problem. I've been seeing one for years!" I said, hanging up the phone.

I made an appointment with Dr. Ross the following day. I shared what I had been experiencing, and he delivered his diagnosis with clarity. "Jeanie, you have what's called *steroid psychosis*. It means that your body reacted to this medication by placing you in a state of manic depression."

"I don't feel depressed, Dr. Ross."

"What you feel is manic. You need to stop taking the pills immediately, but it will not be without side effects. Since the drug caused you to feel high, I'm certain you will most likely crash. There's no way to prepare you for it."

As always, my doctor spoke the truth. By the following day, the excruciating pain in my forehead spread across my eyes, joining the seething pain across the back of my head and neck, and blinding me. I kept a cold cloth over my face, as I felt too sick to move. The word "crash" sufficed to describe my condition.

After sleeping for days, I woke up feeling a resurrection of sorts. Thankful to be alive, I felt all my threats of death had been erased.

Years later, Dr. Evergreen told me he had been able to diagnose a patient suffering similar symptoms due to my encounter with Prednisone. "Jeanie, sometimes that's how doctors learn."

I couldn't help but wonder if Jill and Dr. Ross had learned anything from me over the years. The following experience sheds some light on that question.

By April 1991, I rarely saw Dr. Ross and hardly felt like his patient any longer. Only seven months earlier, I had declared my independence, though still welcoming any excuse to see him. I had a small birthday gift for him and called ahead to ask if I could bring it to his office. "Jeanie, I will be on call so my schedule will be busy, but if you don't mind waiting, I'm sure I can squeeze you in between patients."

It seemed so long ago that I appeared on his weekly schedule. Now, I felt confident and healed. I knew he would be proud of me.

We don't often get a warning signal before pain or tragedy strikes. Unprepared, we deal with it the best we can.

Arriving April 11, 1991, to deliver the present, I took a seat in the all-too-familiar waiting room.

I'm glad for the wait. It will give my heart a chance to stop beating so fast. I can't wait to see the look on Dr. Ross's face when he unwraps the framed picture.

There were reasons I wanted my doctor to have the picture which had previously hung on my wall. One of those reasons would be to remember me.

The following events took place, but *they weren't his fault.* I wasn't there to pay any money this time. I watched as his over-six-foot frame and bald head came through the door into the waiting room and for the first time in my life...he didn't recognize me. He did not acknowledge me.

I sat frozen, unsure what to think. *Maybe he didn't see me. Was that possible? Maybe he had other patients on his mind.*

During the next hour, I felt like I'd been shot with a revolver at close range. It may have happened when he entered the first time and left without a word. Or it could've occurred when he came through the door a second time, barely glancing my way. I'm sure the wound had been inflicted by the third time he appeared. I had no breath to speak. Speechless.

Viewing me as a stranger, Dr. Ross said, "I'm running about fifteen minutes behind today. Do you have an appointment?"

I couldn't dodge the bullet or escape the pain. It felt like I'd been shot and was surrounded by a pool of blood. It must be oozing from my gut.

The receptionist never spoke to me. The other patients didn't say a word.

I must be okay because Dr. Ross didn't see the wound or the blood, so it wasn't his fault.

Unsure I could walk, talk, or stand, I managed to do all three. Picking up the birthday present I had taken such trouble to wrap while sliding his card into my purse, I slipped away without being noticed. I felt ashamed to think I could've been special. *What made me think my gift would be special? Someone special doesn't get ignored or forgotten.*

Numb, cold, and puffy-eyed, I could still feel the tears on my cheeks. *All the wounds are invisible, so it wasn't his fault.*

160

Returning home, I unwrapped the present and hung it back on my wall. The saddest part about invisible wounds is that it's hard to determine if they're anyone's fault.

The following day Libby said, "By the way, Mom, Jill called you, and you're supposed to return her call."

"It would have been nice if you had informed me earlier, Libby," I said irritated. "It will be too late to reach her today and I will have to wait till Monday to see what she wanted."

"Sorry, Mom," Libby replied flippantly, not grasping how disappointed I felt.

I didn't expect my eleven-year-old daughter to understand the level of rejection or abandonment I would have to deal with during a weekend of waiting.

Monday arrived, and Jill called to inform me that she had not made a call to me on Friday. I had also made no call to her. Hearing her voice, I wanted to see her and made an appointment.

After a difficult but helpful session with Jill, I decided to be brave and drop off the picture I had intended to give Dr. Ross. Seeing it on my wall again only brought back painful memories, so I planned to slip it to his receptionist and be on my way.

I no sooner opened the door to his office than his secretary recognized me and walked my way. "Jeanie, did you receive the apology from Dr. Ross?"

Suddenly, it occurred to me that it was his phone call that had slipped Libby's mind. Not a call from Jill.

Looking me straight in the eye, she said, "Jeanie, you looked so different in the waiting room that Dr. Ross did not recognize you. After you left, he realized who you were and remembered the arrangements he'd made with you. He asked me to call you and apologize for him, knowing your feelings must be hurt."

Her words brought tears to my eyes: I took them as a compliment. I was different. I had once been a weekly patient he took care of. His failure to recognize me signified my strength without him but it still seemed sad to no longer be part of his life. I never wanted that. Never.

I now presented the gift—a picture of a child—to him with an expression of gratitude: "Thank you for helping me grow up."

Dr. Ross looked clueless as he opened it, asking, "How did we help you grow up?"

I remember feeling bewildered that he missed that aspect of our relationship.

Only two months later, I would face a different type of goodbye. Mom died of congestive heart failure at seventy-eight. My parents had been married only a month short of fifty years.

Dealing with her death presented me with new challenges, including lack of sleep.

"Jeanie, I'm sending you to Dr. Ross's office to speak to him about some medication to help you sleep and cope with the depression after losing your mom," Jill said. I sensed her concern for me.

Not the least bit interested in medication, I always looked

forward to seeing Dr. Ross. It seemed each time I distanced myself from therapy something drew me back. It wouldn't be long before my relationship with my doctor and therapist reached seven years in duration.

I sat next to Dr. Ross so he could explain the medication and his purpose in prescribing it.

I didn't want medication. I wasn't crazy. Mom never took anything, and she was the one with the mental-health issues. I entered the psychiatric hospital years ago because Mom had problems! This is messed-up.

Within a week I called my psychiatrist. "Dr. Ross, I don't want to take the pills you prescribed for me. I'm sorry. Please don't be mad. It just doesn't feel right, and I'm afraid of the side effects."

"Jeanie, this is entirely your decision. I am not disappointed in you. We can discuss how you are feeling the next time I see you," he said calmly. "It'll be okay." His reassuring words meant a great deal to me.

It would be a decade before I discovered the genetic illness Mom passed on to me, through no fault of her own.

I had a dream after she died. She looked beautiful in the body she had as a younger woman.

Sitting on a hillside, she smiled at me. There appeared to be a river between us that couldn't be crossed. The image seemed real and left me with a peaceful feeling.

I hoped I would remember the good things more than the bad. But it seemed the times she had made me promise to forget were the only memories that surfaced.

Before Mom drew her last breath, I saw a completely different side of her relationship with my dad. He became affectionate, attentive, and present. We would talk about which one of her daughters she wanted to live with. Her last words to me were "I never knew it could take so long to die."

Bye, Mom. I can't promise I won't remember, but I can promise to forgive. See you in Heaven!

"Time to Say Goodbye"

Words / music: Jeanie Connell, 1988

It's time to say goodbye again.
It's time to say goodbye, my friend.
In life through changes we must try
To learn to say goodbye.

>*We only find new hellos*
>*As we let the past doors close.*

It's time to say goodbye again.
It doesn't mean my love will end.
Seeing you—don't know where or when,
But always you'll be my friend.

>*Where are the words to tell you what you've meant?*
>*Where are the hours that we've so dearly spent?*
>*Where will the love go if we move apart?*
>*Can it stay? Can it grow? Can it live evermore in my heart?*

It's time to say goodbye again.
It's time to say goodbye, my friend.
In life through changes, we must try
To learn to say goodbye.
As life brings changes, I will try...But why must we say goodbye?

Listen to this song at jeanieconnell.org / music.

Chapter 19
LET IT GO

"Babe, I don't know why you continue to believe you need them!" Michael spoke with intensity. "I have listened to you promise week after week that you will no longer return to see Jill and Dr. Ross, and you consistently break that promise. Once upon a time you needed their help. That time is over."

Since Dr. Ross and Jill never shared the same appointment with me, I asked if that would be possible. "Dr. Ross, can I meet with both you and Jill at the same time? Would you think about it?" I inquired in my most adult, responsible tone.

"I will consult Jill," he answered. "Jeanie, you either need to do therapy or stop therapy."

Stop therapy? What? His words sounded so cold-hearted. So harsh. Besides, what did my doctor mean by "do therapy"? I was showing up. I was paying money. What more did he want from me?

My next scheduled appointment with Jill found Dr. Ross joining us halfway through the session. I smiled to see them together in the same room. That would be a first and a last.

"Would you sit next to each other so I can take a picture?" There were no smartphones then, so I brought my small camera loaded with film and paid to have it developed at a drug store. The much-cherished photograph got lost or was misplaced but the snapshot is lodged in my memory forever. Maybe this is what Jill meant when she said I would have them in my head one day.

Wondering if they understood my fears about letting them go, I wanted to hear them acknowledge my courage. To call me brave.

Dr. Ross began, "Jeanie, let me give you an idea of the work Jill and I have done with you over the years. Can you imagine that when you walk into our office there is a stage? You are the one who gets on that stage and acts out whatever thoughts and feelings you have. The script is entirely yours. It is our job to listen and pay attention to what you show us on that stage," he explained.

This sounded like new information. I needed to let that marinate.

"I know I have to end therapy someday, but I don't want it to be the end of my relationship with you and Jill," I reasoned. "Why can't I continue to see you sometimes?"

"Jeanie, that isn't the way therapy works," Dr. Ross explained patiently. "If Jill and I have done our job, you will be able to live a healthy lifestyle without us."

Those were the words I dreaded. Without us.

I gave a great deal of consideration to Dr. Ross's definition of therapy—and *I didn't agree!* First, I didn't walk into their office to get on a stage. I paid a lot of money to unlock my secrets and be as real as I knew how to be. I came to share thoughts and feelings that I didn't feel safe to share with anyone else. If this invisible stage existed, I didn't play all the parts myself.

I recently read a quote that said teenagers send and receive over 2,200 text messages a month. One girl who received over 6,400 texts remarked, "I would die without it!"

That is how I felt about the hours I spent with my psychiatrist and therapist.

In contrast, everything I heard from God had the same theme: *Let it go!*

Michael wasn't the only one telling me. I heard it from radio messages, Christian speakers, and sermons: *Let it go! Let it go! Let it go!* The words were clearly aimed in my direction.

Maybe God chased me down the way He did Jonah in the story of Jonah and the Whale. I didn't want to hear His instruction. If my creator had an answering machine, I felt certain his current message would be: "Jeanie, it's Me, God, speaking: Let it go!"

Arguing with God, I reminded Him of a famous song by Michael W. Smith "Friends Are Friends Forever."

I blurted out to my psychiatrist as we walked back to his office, "Dr. Ross, do you believe that Jesus is the Son of God?" His answer reassured me that our relationship could be forever.

I can do this. I can stop therapy. I will stop. I am almost ready to stop therapy. I am not able to stop.

I had unanswered questions and longings that my family and friends could not satisfy.

Jill was in her new office where Dr. Ross worked and needed to step out of the room. I grabbed my chart off her desk and began reading it. Returning, she looked angry and demanded that I hand it back to her. "Jeanie, that is not your property. Please give it to me."

Countering back, I asked, "Why is it your property when it is all about me?" Boldly I read aloud from the file with my name, "Previous visit: patient did not request a goodbye hug."

Indignant, I handed over the chart and said, "Fine! I don't care about your hugs anyway! Ever! I don't even need them!" *My heart hurt, and I wanted to cry.*

During our next appointment, Jill said, "Jeanie, I have to take care of a matter with another patient before we can start."

My response seemed to shock her. "I'd be happy to wait outside in the waiting area till you are finished."

Returning shortly, Jill thanked me and told me she appreciated my understanding. After years of getting acquainted with C.J., I allowed her to communicate with me, the adult. I remember one day asking her about the possibility of a bipolar diagnosis. Her response put an end to the discussion: "Jeanie, you do not have everything you read about in the medical textbooks."

Strangely, I don't remember looking anything up in medical textbooks, including possible side effects for a prescription. "Fine!" I replied, having the last word.

After a hundred broken promises, I would hear Michael say the words I feared: "Babe, if you continue to return to therapy, knowing how strongly I feel about this, we are done."

Michael and our children were my world. He never gave me a reason to doubt his love for me. I didn't want to let him down. Could I face this ultimatum?

C.J. only existed inside of me, the adult. She had grown to trust Jill and Dr. Ross exclusively. They had skin on. She could touch and hug them and make memories she couldn't remember as a little girl in her childhood. Despite this deep longing to be loved and taken care of, I had to take the lead. My adult decisions rested with me.

Meanwhile, dear friends were providing financial backing for me to record my second CD (then cassette), *Roots*. Seven years from my last recording, my dream looked as if it would turn into a reality in 1992. My producer and I spent three days in Asheville, North Carolina, at Hear! Hear! Studio to complete the project.

During the advertising phase, I set off late for my appointment with Dr. Ross. Speeding down the highway, I prayed I would not miss my scheduled sixty minutes. After our session, I felt numb and depressed. *Why do my emotions stay bottled up inside me in their office and burst forth inside my car when I'm alone?*

Before I returned home, I sat for a while, collecting myself and drying my tears. Out of nowhere, I noticed another car leaving the parking lot. I knew I had the last appointment in Dr.

Ross's schedule, so when I saw a man coming from the building in my peripheral vision, I became curious to know if my psychiatrist was driving the exiting car. I wanted to know…but I didn't. My automobile seemed on autopilot as I stayed a safe distance behind the car, never getting close enough to see who sat behind the steering wheel. I followed the car off the expressway and into a neighborhood unfamiliar to me. Abruptly, it turned into a driveway and disappeared behind the house.

Again, I sat pondering, *Could my doctor and therapist possibly live inside that house? How will I ever know? I may now have information that is none of my business.*

I had no intention of being manipulative, let alone a stalker, but the definition fit. I scribbled down the address and faced the hour's drive home. It wouldn't be long before I accidently learned the truth.

"Let It Go"

Words/music: Jeanie Connell, 1992

There isn't any magic, no certain kind of plan,
There isn't any make believe, no magic fairy land.
There isn't anyone that's real to take the feelings I must feel.
I find the only peace I know is to listen when my Father says:
"Let it go. Let it go. Let it go, trust the Lord and let it go."

I wanted someone I could trust, somebody I could see.
If only there were someone safe to come and rescue me.
I've had to learn that I'm the place, inside of me with God I'm safe.
There is no other way to grow than to listen when my Father says, "Let it go."
Ask the Lord...then let it go.

Chapter 20
NEW BEGINNINGS

Nothing says new beginning better than the thrill of being in a studio with talented musicians and recording ten original songs. My producer, a multi-talented musician, made a huge impact on my life.

As the *Roots* recording came into existence, I made some flyers introducing the story behind the music. The songs were tied to my healing, so I shared them whenever possible.

I took one of the flyers and mailed it to the address of the mystery driver, having no idea what might come of it, hoping whoever opened it would assume the flyers had gone out to the entire neighborhood. I never anticipated what would happen next.

The following week during my appointment with Dr. Ross he commented, "It seems you're making headway with your music. I think I saw a flyer on our counter about *Roots*."

Take me now, Lord!! I don't deserve to live! My thoughts were racing: *How will I ever explain what I've done or how I found their address? Would they ever forgive me?*

Shock and panic set in as I sat frozen in silence, while guilt washed over me in waves. *I am in deep trouble. Deep.*

Clearly, I had overstepped my boundaries, and for certain I had crossed theirs. I felt sick inside, eager to end our session and undeserving of my customary hug. Something unpleasant awaited me. My only recourse bore a resemblance to confession with consequences.

I lived in agony until my next appointment with my therapist. "Jill, I have something to tell you, and I know you will be mad," I began, easing into it. Only in hindsight did I realize I should have handled the situation differently.

"As long as you are not going to tell me you have slashed the tires on my car, I think I will be okay," she responded. Those words brought utter dismay. Jill didn't know me at all if she thought I could do anything like that! I could never purposely hurt her or Dr. Ross.

"So…uh…about a week ago, after my appointment with Dr. Ross, I followed an unknown car out of the parking lot. I totally didn't see who drove the vehicle and suddenly, in a strange neighborhood, the car disappeared. For reasons I can't explain, even to myself, I wrote down the address and mailed one of my music flyers to it. The last time I saw Dr. Ross he mentioned my flyer and I figured out what happened. I know where you live."

Feeling guilty and ashamed, I said, "I'm sorry," numerous times.

Now the unbelievably shocking part: Jill did not appear to be angry. She looked calm, even peaceful. *How could this be? I deserved to be yelled at, reprimanded, and looked at with disdain.* This reaction left me confused. Obviously, she expected my confession to be much worse. The discussion ended. Over.

In retrospect, I made one crucial mistake. I failed to ask if I could be the one to relate the incident to Dr. Ross. Big. Mistake.

Before Dr. Ross heard anything from me, Jill passed it on. Trust me when I say it lost something in the translation.

My psychiatrist responded to me with several emotions, none of which was positive. Too angry to discuss it with me, this was the greatest consequence. Worse than anything I could have imagined, I broke his trust, and I knew it. I felt unworthy of his forgiveness.

My phone calls no longer reached him. The appointment turned out to be a last. Like the last time you tuck in your child who's becoming too old for that kind of attention, or the last time you drive your teen before they get their own license, or the last time you kiss a friend goodbye. The lasts you don't see coming. I stood on the brink of a last that would take me more than two decades to accept.

It's my contention that only one thing can help you over a last, and that is a first.

My first turned out to be the fast I shared in Chapter 1 of this book. I no longer made appointments for psychotherapy. Not with Dr. Ross. Not with Jill. Not with anyone. I guess that means they did their job.

I still longed to see them and talk to them. The Merriam-Webster Dictionary says that "out of sight, out of mind" is used to mean "that a person stops thinking about something or someone if he or she does not see that thing or person for a period of time."[1]

This definition remained contrary to what I thought and felt about Dr. Ross and Jill. Though out of sight, Jill's prediction that they would stay in my head proved all too true.

After Chuck Kraft prayed for me on February 7, 1993 (as I mentioned in Chapter One), I was still making attempts to talk with Dr. Ross or Jill. All attempts failed, until our last phone conversation.

"Dr. Ross, this is Jeanie Connell. I just wondered if I could come and introduce myself to you as an adult rather than the inner child you grew accustomed to?" This was spoken strictly in my adult tone of voice, appealing to Dr. Ross's impartiality. The prospects were looking bleak.

Then the words I never wanted to hear: "Jeanie, you don't seem to be able to stop therapy on your own, so Jill and I are going to help you."

While no words were escaping from my mouth, I heard C.J. screaming inside my mind. *No! No! Please don't say that. I promise I will be good. Please don't make me go! Give me another chance. Anything but this! I don't want your help! No, no, no!* The last words came without warning, as they usually do.

I received the following letters in June 1993:

Jeanie,

Because your therapy is at an end, I won't be answering any more last requests.

Use what you have learned in your work with us and have a good life!

Dr. Ross

June 14, 1993

Dear Jeanie,

Life is a series of hellos and goodbyes. Loss is as inevitable as the setting sun. It is a good idea to accept endings with as much dignity and grace as possible. Goodbye,

Jill

The Merriam-Webster definition for "out of sight, out of mind" would work well for my past counselors.

Preferring the much gentler words of the Argentinian writer Jorge Luis Borges, I've included the words of his poem:

After a while, you learn the subtle difference
Between holding a hand
And chaining a soul,

And you learn that love doesn't
mean leaning, and company
doesn't mean security,

And you begin to learn that kisses
Aren't contracts, and presents aren't promises.

And you begin to accept your defeats
With your head up and your eyes ahead,
With the grace of a man or a woman,
Not the grief of a child.

And you learn to build all your roads
On today, because tomorrow's ground is too
Uncertain for plans.
And futures have a way of falling down
In mid-flight.

After a while, you learn that even sunshine
burns if you get too much.
So, you plant your own garden, and decorate
your own soul, instead of waiting for someone
To bring you flowers.

And you learn that you really can endure,
that you really are strong, that you really do have worth.

And you learn and learn
With every letting go, and with every goodbye,
you learn. [2]

I learned a great deal about goodbyes over the years. Each one was unique. Some were more difficult than others. I'm not sure it ever got easier to let go.

Kyle graduated high school in May 1993 and headed off for four years of college at Appalachian State University. Coming home after exams during his second term of school, he gave us a Christmas we would never forget.

Michael and I got a call from paramedics saying they were using jaws of life to cut open Kyle's car to get him out and transport him to a nearby hospital. They reported the bone sticking out of his flesh but didn't mention if he would survive.

We drove, silently praying, not knowing in what condition we would find our son. He was broken and bruised when we first saw him in the Emergency Room. Doctors moved him to the Intensive Care Unit, and we prayed daily to have him home for Christmas. None of us cared about gifts or decorations. Our family had only one wish, and on Christmas Eve it came true. Kyle faced months of rehab after that and had to take a semester off school. But in the interim, the Lord called Kyle to serve him in ministry as a pastor.

After eleven years in our modest North Carolina home, where Kris began his life, Libby socialized, and Kyle recuperated, we moved to Laurens, South Carolina, as Michael took on leadership of another YMCA. Our sprawling new home honored the Clemson Tigers with orange shag carpeting throughout.

There had once been a swimming pool in the backyard, but the previous owners had it filled with dirt and transformed it with trees, bushes, dog kennels, and a pool house. Kris described it as a "forest." Libby recounted it had "a lot going on." Michael said it resembled "an outdoor greenhouse with wildflowers." We immediately began filling it full of memories.

I still thought about my counselors a great deal, but I lived a busy life as a mom, wife, friend, and songwriter. Libby made friends easily in her new school, but the adjustment she had to make in leaving the community where she grew up proved difficult. Eventually, I faced up to the unthinkable: homeschool. Libby begged me to try and, after I nearly backed out, Michael convinced me I had to follow through on my promise.

Scared to death I would ruin any chances my daughter had to be normal, let alone intelligent, we took on senior English, Math, Bible, French, and History. *Wait for it...* It turned out to be the best year of her education. She, grateful to be schooled at home with flexibility, and I, her mom, thrilled to observe her style of learning and come to understand her more than I ever had. Perfect? No. Would either of us trade that semester for anything? No!

Kris in elementary school had an easier time making friends. Not only in school, which he loved, but in church, the Y, swimming, soccer, etc. We moved him to three different schools by the time he entered kindergarten. He had attended preschool and his first kindergarten in North Carolina and his second kindergarten in South Carolina.

Through some friends in Greenville, South Carolina, we were introduced to a small Episcopal church. Their Tuesday night healing service brought people from all denominations. Before long, we were fully invested in this loving congregation and grew closer to God by leaps and bounds. Kids Church assigned leaders for every aspect of the ministry who worked as a team. Some told Bible stories, some took care of greeting the children, some came up with games, and I led the worship with these K through fifth graders. Michael, me, Libby, and Kris made acquaintances that Michael W. Smith would define as "Forever Friends." Inviting Dr. Kraft and Meg to come and introduce the deliverance prayer ministry through a weekend seminar brought many people and marvelous worship—and, as always, captives were set free!

Months later, Michael and I attended a seminar on Mood Disorders in Myrtle Beach. The speaker from Canada talked about depression, ADHD, bipolar depression, and other disorders. The teaching held great interest for both of us and gave us much to think about.

During lunch Michael said, "Jeanie, I see you in the speaker's description of bipolar."

I responded by saying, "I actually see you in his definition of depression." As we talked further, we made an agreement to explore these conditions with our local doctors to see if they could shed any light on a diagnosis, both of us naïvely thinking this would be an easy fix.

Before we would make our next move out of warm sunshine into freezing winters, Libby would graduate high school in South Carolina in 1997 and head out to explore the world. *How could this child of mine be so eager to let go and take off into the unknown? We were as different as night and day.* She remains generous, kind, close to both of her brothers, and always a gift to me. No one helps me to better understand Michael because they are so much alike.

"New Beginnings"

Words/music: Jeanie Connell, 1993

New beginnings, new beginnings,

We're gathered here to see an outward sign of new beginnings.

Not everything we leave behind must cause us tears.

We learn that change becomes more graceful through the years.

There comes a time to say goodbye to one-and-only.

We can accept new love and joy in place of lonely.

Letting the door close on our past invites the present.

Looking ahead, our spirit shines; we're effervescent.

Let's look for inward signs that need a new beginning:

Maybe our minds, maybe our hearts,

Maybe our lives just need a fresh start.

Maybe our eyes no longer see

The miracles taking place in you and me.

Lord, let this day be just the start of new beginnings.

Let this day be just the start of new beginnings, new beginnings, new beginnings.

Only Jesus Christ can give…New Beginnings.

Listen to this song at jeanieconnell.org/music.

Chapter 21
LITTLE GIRL

Before I left Salisbury, North Carolina, my first book, *I Can Grow Up: All I Ever Needed to Know About Being Grown-Up I Learned from My Kids*, was published by Rowan Business Forms, Inc. The book related my journey through therapy through the eyes of a child.

Dr. Ross and Jill's reparenting skills taught me simple truths, which I wrote down in a large sketch pad. I would look for magazine pictures that gave visual expression to the words I'd written. I kept the spiral pad hidden in our china cabinet, showing no one. I loved looking at my notebook and adding pages along with pictures that represented the following ideas:

- *Other people are as special as me.*
- *Feelings are something God understands.*
- *Angry feelings don't have to hurt other people.*
- *I can like myself when I make mistakes.*
- *I can change me; I cannot change other people.*
- *Safe is something very important that everyone needs to feel.*

- *With enough loving, I can grow up.*[1]

Slowly, I began replacing the magazine pictures with photographs of our own children and their friends. An artist friend, Sherry W. Thurston, drew a sketch of Kris for the front cover of my notebook.

While I was working as Program Coordinator for the Battered Women's Shelter, I met Rick Hardesty at Rowan Business Forms, the company that printed the first thousand copies.

In the book. I acknowledged my family, friends, Dr. Kraft, and God, while omitting any mention of Jill and Dr. Ross, who inspired the entire project.

Responding kindly when I mailed them the book, Jill said she enjoyed seeing the photos of our children.

I wouldn't deny that our three children taught me a lot. However, this book expressed what I learned from C.J. hiding inside of me, who showed up behind the closed door of therapy.

The following excerpt from *Child Sexual Abuse: A Hope for Healing* (Hancock & Mains, 1987) explains the importance that a counseling relationship can have for a season of our life:

> The counselor's work is to help us see through our own rationalizations, denials, and our projections, our isolating of feelings from events, our selective repressions—much of which the healthy, truth-loving mind can do for itself.

However, when a human being has grown into adulthood without an emphasis on truth, without facing reality as it is rather than as he wishes it to be, without coming to terms with the natural bent to self-deception, self-awareness is much more difficult.

The survivors of child sexual abuse are often raised in an atmosphere of untruth, and consequently, many have not achieved the resources for ongoing development. Emotional development has been severely disrupted, and victims often feel chained by their childhood circumstances. They feel they have nowhere to go, and nothing worth living for. When abuse occurred in early childhood, the establishment of trust, both in oneself, and in others, has been short-circuited.

In many cases of child sexual abuse, the ability to cope is so severely damaged that a good counselor is very often part of God's provision in the healing process. Very often the therapist becomes a surrogate emotional parent during certain periods of therapeutic work. A pastor becomes a father substitute, a friend becomes a nurturing mother who cares, who is present, and says to us the words we have never heard but need so badly. The temptation in these relationships is to fixate on them because of past deprivation and to want to cling, to own, to hold. Skilled professionals will try to prevent the transference from getting stuck in the negative fashion, and those who are needy must teach themselves to recognize the relationships for what they are—gifts given for healing times rather than as permanent relational institutions.[2]

My birthday, December 28, 1997, found me wanting only one gift: to be seen by Jill and Dr. Ross as an adult, no longer the child they cared for. I imagined how surprised and delighted they would be to see how I had changed, behaving and reasoning like a mature adult. Surely, they would be pleased to know their years of work with me had not been in vain.

(Does this scenario sound familiar?)

I didn't inform Michael of my three-hour drive to North Carolina. Our kids knew I would be gone for the day, so *happy birthday to me!*

No longer under my psychiatrist and therapist's professional care, I felt no guilt in knowing their private address. I made a birthday card explaining why I'd come, hoping to place it in their hands when I arrived.

Singing and in high spirits as I drove, I felt only slightly nervous about the unknown. The weather was icy-cold but there was no snow on the ground. I parked on their street several houses away, next to the curb. A large, leafy tree stood directly outside their house, which made me feel sheltered. I looked up into the sky and prayed: *Jesus, I know Your promise not to leave me alone. I love you, Father God, and after all these years I have no doubts that You love me too. Thank You for healing me. Four years feels like a resurrection of sorts. What better birthday present could I ask for than this?*

Getting out of the car, I found the courage to walk up the few concrete steps to their front door. Jill answered with a quiet sound that made me consider turning back rather than waiting on their doorstep. The look on her face communicated skepticism, not welcome.

She left me standing outside while she turned and went inside again.

I backed down the steps and waited, clutching my homemade birthday card, and still feeling sheltered by the large tree.

When Dr. Ross came out of the house and walked toward me, there was an unfamiliar expression on his face I had not seen before. No hint of the smile that used to greet me week after week for seven years. No kindness. No compassion. No mercy.

His words were defensive and carefully chosen, concise, filled with anger, matched only by the glare on his face. "Jeanie, you are *not* my patient. You are *not* my child. You are *not* my friend. Get off my property!"

Amazed that I could still stand, I walked to my car. The night seemed to have grown suddenly darker. The carefully written card fell out of my hand, landing on frozen, brown grass. If I had been thrown to the ground, I wouldn't have noticed. The anger I provoked—tragic. The rejection—tangible.

There were no thoughts of suicide or desperate attempts for attention. I had changed.

This interaction was the *last* I never expected. Those were the last words I would ever hear my psychiatrist speak to me. I've replayed them in my mind for more than twenty years.

Arriving home, I fell into Michael's arms and confessed where I'd gone and why. He showed me kindness. Compassion. Mercy. As he held me, he said, "It's their loss, babe. They only remember who you once were. You have come so far."

The following poem gives word pictures and emotions to breaking a habit:

"Autobiography in Five Short Chapters"
From Portia Nelson, *There's a Hole in My Sidewalk*,
copyright 1993.

Chapter I
I walk, down the street.
There is a deep hole in the sidewalk.
I fall in.
I am lost…I am hopeless.
It isn't my fault.
It takes forever to find a way out.

Chapter II
I walk down the same street.

There is a deep hole in the sidewalk.

I pretend I don't see it.

I fall in again.

I can't believe I am in the same place.

But it isn't my fault.

It still takes a long time to get out.

Chapter III

I walk down the same street.

There is a deep hole in the sidewalk.

I see it is there.

I still fall in…it's a habit.

My eyes are open.

I know where I am.

It is my fault.

I get out immediately.

Chapter IV

I walk down the same street.

There is a deep hole in the sidewalk.

I walk around it.

Chapter V

I walk down another street.[3]

"Little Girl"
Words/music: Jeanie Connell

Little girl, little girl, you are safe, you are Mine!
You are so precious and so loving, for you I'll always have the time.
Oh, little girl, little girl, come and sit at My feet.
You've finally learned there is no other that you'll ever need to seek.
I'll feel your pain, I'll hear your joy, I'll see your smiles, I'll dry your tears.
And you can trust Me with your secrets, whether dreams or plans or fears.

My daughter you have got the faith! Now go in peace,
I set you free from your suffering.
Don't be afraid, now just believe, this is the time I want you to sing!
Why all the crying? The child's alive now
With a song she has to bring.
She knows her Father, she is awake now: little girl—arise and sing!

Oh, little girl, little girl, help others see their child within.
Without dependence and total trusting, the battle's hopeless, they'll never win.

Lift up your eyes, look in My face, there is a joy I've longed to see.

So many times, I've held you closely and watched you struggle to be free.

But I stood firm because I care, because I love, because I know

That as you suffered, and as I broke you,

You could be strong now, as I taught you how to grow.

I had to break you. You would be strong now, as I taught you how to grow.

Listen to this song at jeanieconnell.org/music.

Chapter 22
BUTTERFLY

"Hey, babe, I got a call from the YMCA in Warren, Pennsylvania. They are hiring a CEO and invited me to interview for the position," Michael announced. "Let's pray about it, okay?"

When it came to a new job or a new home, we prayed until we agreed on a decision. The temptation to see Jill and Dr. Ross no longer existed but living nine hours away made no difference to the desires of my heart. I missed them. They were my memories, and I didn't want to forget them.

As Michael became the YMCA Director (CEO), I answered an ad in the local newspaper to lead a contemporary worship service at Grace United Methodist Church. I loved working with this talented team of seven musicians and had prayed for a name to set it apart. The subject line from another worship leader in Pennsylvania read: "Grace to Grace." That was it! The name I'd been waiting for.

Sadly, less than two years later, I announced my resignation because *I believed God asked me to.* It would take some time to realize I let them and myself down. My moods fluctuated along with my decisions. I never grew tired of my responsibilities at the church, only conflicted about the voice of God and how to obey it.

Making a trip back to North Carolina to spend time with friends, I secretly hoped the door might open so that I could see Jill and Dr. Ross. My call to their offices reached only the receptionist and confirmed that the door remained closed.

Our marriage faced great obstacles at this time, including Michael's health. His depression seemed pronounced, while my emotions skyrocketed when they weren't plummeting.

I enrolled in an online course through AACC (American Association of Christian Counselors) called *Caring for People God's Way*. I became trained in lay counseling on several topics. One of my instructors, a therapist in Philadelphia, taught on the subject of sexual abuse survivors. I decided to make an appointment and drove six hours to meet her. The fact that she treated me like a patient, rather than a student, offended me. Paying full price for my hour with her insulted me. My lay counseling course would allow me to listen to people free of charge. I no longer thought of therapy as rent-a-friend. The profession is made up of men and women who have spent a large amount of money to pay for each year of medical training.

The friends who came alongside of me during my ten years of counseling were as important as my doctors and therapists. They prayed for my healing, encouraged me, and believed in me.

During the four years I lived in Warren, Pennsylvania, I

developed a lasting relationship with one of those friends. Meg Butler and I met at a church conference and knew from the start we were kindred spirits. We both played guitar and sang, and Meg also had the ability to write music down, which I had never witnessed. She would listen to my original songs and write them down on paper, with a music staff, tempo, time signature, and refrains. Making it look as simple as writing a letter to a friend, she shared this amazing gift by writing down more than thirty of my songs.

Meg relocated to Franklin, Tennessee.

A friend from Pennsylvania drove with me to Nashville to attend my AACC graduation at Gaylord Opryland Resort & Convention Center. Having never completed college with cap and gown, this ceremony meant a great deal to me.

Meg drove to Opryland to attend my graduation as well. My sister Kathy's son worked at a restaurant nearby, so we celebrated there. I loved all that I learned about the counseling process from those who sat on the other side of the desk. Doors in our community were opened to train other Christians how to listen to those who are hurting. Lay counseling was made available in local churches. *Caring For People God's Way* spread through our community as I shared the video course with others.

When I wasn't traveling or learning about counseling, my home and garden was my sanctuary. Our Pennsylvania home on the corner lot, built in 1902, had a flower garden that caught the eye of all who passed by. The colors were breathtaking, and when the tulips were finished showing off, another flower would appear to take their place. This spectacular floral array, credited to the previous owners, was now ours to enjoy.

Sitting upstairs on our four-poster bed, my "Butterfly" song came floating into my thoughts like the very creature itself. (I have this song printed at the end of this chapter.)

Collage with butterflies – ROOTS: God's Heartstrings, 2000

A favorite retreat spot just outside of Warren was Olmstead Manor. I don't have words to describe its exquisite beauty! Butterflies were drinking from the flowers, and the Earth was singing nature's song—just for me. I was alone at this gorgeous place, and I penned the following words:

"All I Needed to Know About Freedom, I Learned from a Butterfly"

The last time I sensed God speaking to me I had stepped back from my busy pace. I heard Him saying, "Wait. Wait with Me." The established church can become as busy and hectic as any place in the world. I had taken almost no opportunities to "Be still and know..." I dreaded the quiet, fearing boredom or discomfort. In truth, it offers new life.

Research shows it takes twenty-one days to make a habit. Experience shows it takes much longer to break one. Some habits are harmful while others bring about much-needed change. On February 7, 1993, in a chapel I prayed and asked God to change me. Over the next seven years, I tried to make choices to obey God's voice, rather than follow my feelings.

On a single day in October 1999, I recognized an inner change like a butterfly emerging from its cocoon. A change in thoughts and emotions strikingly different from the past. I had to question: How did it happen?

Unlike drawing comparisons to a butterfly, I felt I was a butterfly! I felt like a new creature. Beautiful and transformed.

The final sentence as I finished a novel read: "Go and be as the butterfly." The following morning a friend's email said, "God transforms us—a metamorphosis actually—like a caterpillar into a butterfly." I knew the voice of the Holy Spirit had spoken to me.

During a time of quiet reflection, I stood in the sunshine with a Bible in my hands. A ladybug landed on the cover, and I began to block its path with my finger. It caused the bug to go in a different direction. As it moved around, I realized God can guide and direct my path in a similar way. When something prevents me from going one way, I can choose another path. Eventually, the ladybug came to the outer corner of the Bible and with no right or left options, spread its wings to fly! God speaks through His Word, His children, and His creatures, big and small.

"Butterfly"
Words/music: Jeanie Connell, 1999.

CHORUS: I am new, and I don't know how it happened
I am new and I'm not sure how I got here.
I am new; I believe in miracles 'cause
I'm a butterfly today.

I stepped out of my home to take a look around,
I felt much higher up, not crawling on the ground.
An ugly brown cocoon I saw was left behind
How dark it must have been, now a light was finally mine!

*CHORUS

The thought of how I'd changed, the graceful way I feel
The beauty of my life, how could it all be real?
I knew it took me years to shed that old cocoon,
Yet in a single day my winter turned to June!

*CHORUS

Listen to this song at jeanieconnell.org/music.

Chapter 23
ILLUSION

It was cold in November 2000 when Michael picked me up from the airport after I'd been traveling. Returning from Winter Springs, Florida, I could not have imagined the conversation that awaited me.

"Jeanie, I need you to listen carefully," my husband began. He didn't appear panicked or particularly stressed.

"I had a slight cardiac arrest during my work out at the YMCA today."

Did he just say what I thought he said? How does someone have a slight heart attack? Either they have a heart attack, or they don't.

In seconds, I realized his attempts to downplay the experience so I wouldn't overreact or become frightened.

"I told the ambulance driver that I couldn't go to St. Vincent's Hospital in Erie, Pennsylvania, until I picked up my wife from the airport."

Aside from your heart issues, you have lost your mind! No one asks the ambulance to wait for a more convenient time! I imagined the trained paramedics were not happy with Michael's request.

In a daze somewhere between reality and illusion, I thought, *Is this real? Am I facing a "last"?*

Michael dropped me off at home and talked to Kris about these events. He didn't want our son to feel afraid. Michael expressed his love to him and remained calm. "Hey kiddo, I'm going to the hospital in Erie for a few days. Help your mom out, okay? I love you."

Just in the last year, we lost Michael's mom. Eileen Connell, a fighter in overcoming breast cancer, heart failure, and the loss of her spouse, succumbed to leukemia. We were grateful that standing next to her hospital bed, we witnessed her *last* peaceful breath.

Now, unexpectedly, seeing paramedics hook Michael up to an IV feed containing nitroglycerin and driving him ninety minutes in an ambulance to an unknown hospital, left me feeling insecure.

During his hospital stay, I ended up in the small apartment accommodation provided for those who had a family member awaiting surgery. Unpacking my duffle bag, I came across a book by Stormie Omartian, *The Power of a Praying Wife.* I began interceding for my husband immediately.

After tests were run, the doctors determined that Michael had five arteries that were between 99 and 100% obstructed. He would undergo a quintuple bypass, considered the most intricate form of heart surgery.

When I visited Michael's bedside in the hospital, we were able to remain serene in the crisis. We searched for a scripture to comfort us. When I opened my Bible, we read the words, "O Lord my God, I called to You for help, and You healed me" (Psalm 30:2).

We believed in Almighty God. The God who heals.

Before I returned from Florida, I visited Northland church and sensed the Lord speaking to me during the prayer service, calling me to take part in a ministry team to Namibia, southwestern Africa. The entire congregation bowed and answered for themselves whether God had asked them to pray, give, or go. In all my years of church membership, I had never felt called to missions. This seemed new. With my eyes closed, I could see Kris (then thirteen) going with me. This first would not be the last time that missions would have a place in my life.

"Honey," I began my conversation with Michael before his date for surgery, "when I attended Northland in Florida, a man named Josh from South Africa asked the congregation to pray about being part of a mission team to his country. I believe God spoke to my heart about going this summer and taking Kris."

Could this even possibly be God's timing? My husband just suffered a heart attack, and I'm telling him Kris and I need to raise $5,000 to go to Namibia in a matter of months!

As I continued to pray and seek God's direction, it seemed I received His confirmation more than once.

Kris and I attended a local youth rally together and explained the vision for Africa. Several of the teens wanted to support our trip. All the necessary funds poured in when we were given the opportunity to share about our trip with local churches and at other community outreach events.

Kris and I did travel to Africa with a party of men, women, and college students in July 2001, only eight months after Michael's surgery. I had no more illusions of how people in a third world country lived. I experienced reality as I had never known or imagined it. It became a life-changing trip for both me and our son.

Shortly after Michael's heart attack, he received a call from the YMCA in Fayetteville, North Carolina. "Mike," the president of the board said, "would you consider coming to interview for the position of Executive Director?"

Declining, he explained his recent heart attack and current recovery. End of subject. Period.

Several months later, the Y board president called again, "Mike, how are you feeling?"

Michael replied, "Actually, I'm recuperating much faster than I expected. Thanks for asking."

"We have interviewed several candidates and the board keeps coming back with your name. Is it possible you feel healthy enough to reconsider this position?"

"Jeanie and I will pray," Michael responded gratefully. The more job offers and new homes, the more prayer.

Instinctively, I knew my husband wanted to accept this position. It wouldn't be the first time I followed his lead and moved…or the *last.*

In February 2002, we sold our beautiful home, leaving behind memories both happy and sad and purchased a home in Fayetteville, North Carolina, only minutes from the YMCA.

As Michael became stronger physically, our marriage needed intensive care. ICU. Our brokenness happened over a period of years when we weren't paying attention. We had not given enough tender loving care to our most valuable relationship. We had sought the help of human counselors and failed to go together before the King of our hearts—Jesus.

The following verse showed us what had happened: "My people have committed two sins: they have forsaken Me, the spring of living water, and have dug their own cisterns that cannot hold water" (Jeremiah 2:13).

What a picture. Nowhere in this passage of scripture does God condemn our thirst. The two sins are turning away from Him and turning to other things to satisfy ourselves. During those years in therapy, I wanted to believe that Jill and Dr. Ross could quench my thirst.

After we moved to Fayetteville, we began counseling with a local pastor. As a couple, it seemed helpful in getting our lives back on course. Both Michael and I followed through on our decision to explore medication for bipolar disorder and depression. Michael mentioned it to his current primary physician, and she had no hesitation in prescribing something because of his recent health setbacks.

My experience, much different, proved more complicated. A friend recommended a psychiatrist. Just showing up for the appointment and giving my history felt like a backward step. He confirmed a diagnosis of bipolar disorder type 2 and prescribed a medication used to control seizures. It interfered with my daily exercise and left me groggy, sluggish, and not myself.

My emotions continued to swing, with down days more extreme and good days unpredictable. The wrong medication is almost worse than no medication at all.

Some friends in our new church introduced us to an event called Pilgrimage. Nothing compared to this love encounter with Jesus, shown through the body of Christ. No phones or watches allowed. Truth taught from God's Word. Treats and surprises around every corner and, of course, music. Songs to express our hearts.

As marvelous as the encounter turned out to be, it also exposed the depth of my depression and the emptiness I perceived in our marriage. Ten long years of therapy had taken its toll, chipping away at the trust and intimacy in our relationship.

Our situation reminded me of what Charles Dickens wrote in *A Tale of Two Cities*: "It was the best of times, it was the worst of times, it was the age of wisdom, it was the age of foolishness, it was the epoch of belief, it was the epoch of incredulity, it was the season of light, it was the season of darkness, it was the spring of hope, it was the winter of despair." [1]

Only God knew this described what awaited Michael and me in the coming year. A season of reality.

"Illusion"
Words/music: Jeanie Connell, 2000.
Written for Dr. Ross & Jill.

Were you just an illusion, just an idol form?
Nothing changed for you and yet I had been reborn.
Could you explain my delusion? Thinking I had found
All that I had lost and yet you were not around?
Would you forgive my intrusion? Wanting you to see
Something deep inside of the deepest part of me.
I wanted you to exclusion, nothing else was real.
Only with your help could I learn again to feel.
And yet I found in conclusion...
You were just an illusion.

Listen to this song at jeanieconnell.org/music.

Chapter 24
GIFTS

February 2003—the phone call came from the National YMCA. "Michael, we have a group of people in Panama City, Florida, who would like to establish a Y. Would you be willing to go to Florida and show them what's involved in the process? It should only take a day or so."

Michael, loving the beach and warm weather, agreed to go. Kris (eighth grade) and I joined him. The weather—chilly, rainy, and dreary—turned out to be most unusual for this popular vacation spot.

While Michael met with various individuals, explaining the training and resources needed to launch a YMCA, Kris and I kept busy exploring the town.

Returning home, we gave little thought to our quick trip to Panama City until...the next phone call. "Mr. Connell, we believe the first step in starting a YMCA in Bay County is to hire the Chief Executive Officer. We know of no one better qualified than you."

Somewhat stunned, Michael responded, "Let me pray about this with my wife, and I will get back to you."

My first thoughts were the house in Fayetteville that we had lived in for barely a year. Moving brought dread. Selling our home that we were so blessed to find, looking for a buyer offering a comparable price, not to mention finding the right church. These thoughts were followed by further ones of our recent trip to a dreary, rainy beach and knowing no one. Not one person. Being in the middle of eighth grade in a private Christian school, Kris would need to be homeschooled since it looked as if we would leave mid-semester. But we made the decision to move together. All three of us at the same time. That was a *first*. Our previous moves found me waiting until the house sold, school was over, and loose ends were tied up.

This job offered the same adequate salary as his present position, except Michael had to *raise* the funds before the money would appear in his paycheck.

Like a new church being planted, this Y had no building, no roots, and no staff, and it would require much commitment and energy. Energy from two adults who were already experiencing some burnout.

No longer taking the medication that made me groggy, my moods were off the charts. Michael enjoyed his favorite habitat, the beach, and a generous couple offered to let us live in their beautiful home across from the water while they moved into another one on the same street. We were thankful for these generous friends who allowed us to stay until our previous home sold. We woke up every morning to a breathtaking view. Water. Sand. Stillness. New beginnings. Gifts from God.

214

Kyle and Libby arrived to celebrate Easter with us. We were quickly planted in a friendly church where I became involved in the prayer team. Kris became active in the youth group, made friends, and his faith increased steadily. Another gift.

Was our brokenness healed? No. We were better able to camouflage it.

In June 2003, after closing on our home in North Carolina, we purchased a three-bedroom house in Panama City Beach. About a ten-minute drive from the white sandy beaches, we lived at the end of the street in our friendly neighborhood and things got better…before they got worse. Much worse.

Panama City Beach, Florida—Michael, Jeanie, and eighth-grade Kristofer (in the background), 2003

Finding where to fit in a new city is never easy. Panama City Beach proved to be no exception. We prayed about new schools, jobs, friends…*forever friends.*

Our struggles and challenges reflected the brokenness only God could heal. In 2004, I wrote the following essay to describe in detail our unlikely *gift* from God.

"Get the Divorce"
August 5, 2004

Michael and I, both brought up in the church, believed the Bible to be true. We are about the same age, same race, and neither of our parents had experienced divorce. It seemed our similarities stopped there. He is athletic, I am musical. My love language is words, his is silence. Our three children reflect us in different ways. However, all three of them share Michael's tan complexion, dark hair, and brown eyes, and *love* of sports.

In March 2004, driving home alone, after a time of listening to the Lord, I heard Him say (in His voice inside my mind), *Pull over and get your journal.* As I found a spot in the parking lot, I heard, *Get the divorce. Jesus loves you.* Looking up, I realized I parked next to a Bible supply store. There were large, wooden, red letters on the side of the building that read, "Jesus Loves You." Tears were pouring down my cheeks (not unusual during that season of my life). I knew if I heard God, my response must be obedience.

Some history…Five years previous, I questioned if a divorce would give our marriage a fresh start. A close friend advised me, "That is *never* a step you take without hearing God instruct you." *Could this be God's voice? Was the enemy trying to deceive me? Would I be able to discern a counterfeit voice? If this **is** God's voice, what should I do?*

Talking with Michael, he became angry. When he felt hurt, rejected, accused, or disappointed, he had one emotional response—anger.

We don't believe in divorce. We don't use the word or consider it as an option for our marriage. How could I be hearing this? How do I show my obedience?

Over the next several months, I shared what I'd heard with a few close friends, not necessarily in Florida. Their response? "God hates divorce!"

I know of other things God also hates. Holy Spirit, I need You to help me understand.

Thinking about the story of Abraham when God asked him to sacrifice his son, I realized that it did not call for consultation and asking the advice of friends. If God indeed gave me instruction, it called for my obedience.

On July 21, Michael, Kris, and I had eaten in a restaurant and had a few stops to make on the way home. Michael's angry tone gave off the feeling he was provoked and displeased. I had become so tired of his irritations. Dropping him off at home, I took Kris to a youth retreat on the beach. As I stood in worship surrounded by hundreds of young people, I heard the Lord say, "Jeanie, it's time."

As I turned to leave the crowded room, I saw Kris with his hands raised, worshiping Jesus. A memory I will carry forever.

Returning home, I shared with Michael that I would be calling an attorney the next day, asking for a mediation. Furious, he lashed out with his words. Later, Kris, visibly shaken, asked for a Bible with a concordance. He began searching for something. Soon, he closed the Bible and said, "I understand." I never asked him about it.

Seeing Kris in tears broke my heart. I told him this would feel like a death had taken place. I told him we could trust God to lead us one step at a time. He had questions I couldn't answer.

The following morning, I woke up with a sick feeling, while Kris woke with tears, which were rare for him. Libby called early and became very angry with me. Kyle called later, also angry, but didn't want to discuss it over the phone. He had already planned to come home for a week's vacation.

We had an appointment on July 27, 2004, to end our marriage of thirty-three years.

The Lord seemed to be telling me to go to my dad's house for three days to give Michael space. My friend

Olivia made the seven-hour drive with me to Winter Springs, Florida. Dad and I had a long talk when I arrived. Wanting to understand, he still appeared troubled.

I woke up the next morning hearing the Lord's voice, "Jeanie, you are a woman of faith." I opened my Bible to Proverbs 6 and 7, which mentioned adultery. Both Michael and I had been guilty of turning to other gods and turning away from the Lord.

I suddenly took an aggressive stand against the father of lies! "There is no way that the enemy is gaining any more ground in our marriage!" I had an overwhelming desire to fast and pray. I cried out to God as never before. "Michael Connell will no longer be held captive by our enemy."

I knew Olivia and my dad were also praying.

I heard the Lord telling me to call our children and my two sisters to ask for prayer. Soon, the names of other couples in different states came to mind. Every phone call answered. Every message we sent was the same:

> This is urgent! Michael and I have an appointment with an attorney in three days to end our marriage. Please pray the following:
>
> 1) Deliver both of us from a spirit of adultery. (There had been no infidelity.)
> 2) Break down any/all strongholds of anger in both of us.

3) Release to us our God-given emotions.

4) Please pray for these requests together as a couple.

After sixteen phone calls, including to Chuck Kraft and Meg, the Holy Spirit gave me new direction. "Your prayers have been heard and answered. Give Me thanks and praise before you see the results." The remainder of the day turned out to be restful. Dad took us out to dinner.

The next day, Olivia accompanied me to a nearby church where a group of intercessors were gathered to pray. We joined them and enlisted more prayer support.

Sunday, I heard several messages crafted specifically for me. Northland church had guest speakers: Les and Leslie Parrott spoke about marriage. *Coincidence? No way.* "No human being can complete another, even in marriage," Les shared. I had heard them speak during my graduation in Nashville, years prior.

Olivia and I attended the second worship service at my dad's church in Winter Park, Florida. The topic: Being Misunderstood. Several people I loved and respected judged me based on the limited knowledge they had, rather than offering to pray as we listened for God's voice.

Sunday night, the three of us returned to Dad's church for a message on evangelism using the Ten Commandments. As I listened, the Word of God opened my ears. *God doesn't contradict Himself! Since He hates divorce, we cannot keep the appointment with the attorney on July 27.*

Calling Michael for the first time in three days, I said, "Michael, I don't believe God wants this mediation." We both agreed the appointment needed to be canceled.

"We will lose the money I had to pay," I reminded him. Neither of us cared. We both agreed our marriage needed help. That seemed a first.

"Michael, have you been crying out to the Lord for our marriage?" I asked.

"No way! I figured if God told you to divorce me, He must be on your side, not mine. I have been angry and didn't have anything to say to Him." Again, the anger.

Monday morning found me weeping before the Lord. *How could I have been so blind to the truth, Lord? I don't understand.*

Quietly, I heard Him speak, "Beloved, have you drawn closer to Me in the past three days? Have you continued to hear My voice clearly? You were obedient. Like Abraham, placing the person he loved most on the altar. You also were willing to sacrifice the one you love most. I gave him back."

Tears flowed as I made the phone call to cancel the appointment with the attorney. Olivia and I headed for home with grateful hearts and praises to Jesus. Stopping by Northland church, we bumped into the young pastor who traveled with me to Africa two years prior. Happy to see each other, we spoke. He said, "I am never in this part of the church on a Monday morning." He stopped and prayed for us, "Lord, let Jeanie and Olivia see expressions of God's love for them as they travel."

Not fifteen minutes later, Olivia shouted, "Look!" and pointed upward. As we gazed out the car window, we saw skywriting in process, coming from a small aircraft: *Jesus Loves You! Love, God.* The white letters were clearly legible against the blue background. A thrilling reminder.

Less than thrilling was reconnecting with my husband. He felt like a stranger. We had both been shaken. Our whole family felt the jolt. We needed Jesus to lead us every step of the way. I asked Michael if we could put ourselves before the Lord and His Word, as a couple, for the next seven days, and let Him be our Counselor. We both agreed, not realizing *Our Counselor and Comforter* already had a plan.

At four that morning, in tears, I asked Michael to take me away, just the two of us, getting before the Lord with no disguises. When I woke up, I returned a phone call to a friend. I asked if there was any chance that we could use their condo at the beach. She generously offered it to us for the next several days.

We packed very little and stayed at the beach, not far from home. The enemy wanted us to believe our marriage would end on July 27, 2004. Instead, a new beginning took place as God created a new covenant between us. We felt like a honeymoon couple during those three days. Each day we sat together with our Bible to allow God to be our Counselor. The Lord tells us that His sheep hear His voice.

Both of us brought books to share. I remember resting on the sofas and hearing Michael read about the true commitment of marriage—about serving each other and dying to self.

We already knew marriage could be difficult, now we were learning it took hard work to keep it moving in the right direction.

On day three the *honeymoon* looked different. Michael orders his day by giving permission for his watch to take over. I order my day by letting the *Spirit* lead, regardless of what's on my schedule. Our agendas conflicted.

We both became frustrated. Michael acted like I had a plan to ruin his day. I felt like he wasn't willing to do the things that were important to me. Anger surfaced.

It saddened me to see him stressed, with tension headaches. Softly, I asked, "Don't you want to get rid of the anger that attaches itself to you? It's like a monkey on your back."

Returning to the condo, Michael apologized for his bad mood. I requested he read to me from the Bible. As he began, our *Counselor* joined us. I inquired if Michael wanted to receive prayer. To my surprise he said, "Yes, Jeanie, I am ready to receive a prayer of deliverance."

After eating dinner out, tired, I went to bed and was awakened about ten o'clock by the phone ringing. Considering it might be Chuck Kraft wanting an update, I literally rolled out of bed onto the floor and began to pray. I couldn't hear any conversation from the bedroom, but I stayed on the floor waging war for my husband. *The battle belongs to the Lord.*

Forty-five minutes later, Michael appeared at the bedroom door with his hands extended in the air and saying, "I am free!"

Tears came to my eyes as we both witnessed an answer to our prayers.

Laying down beside me, he said, "The demons were in bundles, Jeanie. Chuck kicked them out. I have to get up and write it down!" (None of this was typical behavior for my husband.) Joining him in the living room, hearing the tone of his voice, and seeing the expression on his face brought back memories of my prayers of deliverance in 1993.

The next day our three kids joined us at the condo near the beach. During lunch, Michael mentioned Chuck Kraft's phone call. Our children could tell it made an impact on their dad. His actions spoke louder than words.

We extended our *counseling* with Jesus to twenty-one

days to form a habit. We both used a Bible study called *A Walk in Repentance* by Steve Gallagher. For years I believed we were waiting on God. The truth was, He waited on us.

Michael wrote the following words just after he gained his newfound freedom.

"I Am Set Free"
July 29, 2004

Tonight, at approximately ten o'clock, I became set free from years of anger, hatred, rejection, bitterness, and fear. Jesus, through Chuck Kraft's prayers, delivered me of anger and hate that had taken up residence in my life since my boyhood. I have been released and have forgiven those who hurt me over years, especially my mom. "Mom, I love you and can't wait to be reunited with you."

As Chuck spoke to the different spirits, my body jerked violently. First anger, then revenge, rejection, bitterness, lust, and the big one, fear, were delivered into Jesus' care. I could see Jesus put them in a box and burn them. Then, in my mind I also saw Him place His hand on my head and say, "You are forgiven, and you are free, free to laugh, and free to be who I created you to be." Then I saw Him smile and sort of fade away.

A peace that I have never experienced came over me.

I thanked Dr. Kraft and then ran in to see Jeanie and tell her I had been set free.

We hugged and she prayed.

Mike Connell

As I thought about what had happened to Michael and me, two verses came to mind:

"Now the Lord is the Spirit, and where the Spirit of the Lord is, there is freedom" (2 Corinthians 3:17).

"So, if the son sets you free, you will be free indeed" (John 8:36).

I never would have considered a near-brush with divorce could be a *gift*.

Another unlikely gift came in September 2004. Driving to North Carolina to visit a close friend, my emotions were off the charts I was elated in song one hour and weeping in sadness the next. Developing some type of virus, I made an appointment to see our previous family doctor. During that visit I asked him a question, "Dr. Evergreen, if possibly you were right fifteen years ago about the bipolar diagnosis, what would you suggest now?"

"Well, Jeanie, I would prescribe a medication and see if you felt better after thirty days. You would need to find a doctor in Florida to continue treatment."

"I understand," I responded. After I shared with a friend before I took the prescription, she prayed that the medication would have no negative side effects. I thought to myself, *That seems like a bold request considering the reaction I've had to drugs in the past.*

Then I remembered God's Word: "Until now you have not asked for anything in my name. Ask and you will receive, and your joy will be complete" (John 16:24 NIV).

I was grateful for her prayer, which became an important part of my story.

Within the thirty days, Michael noticed a positive shift in my moods. I felt balanced in a way I couldn't describe. My kids also noticed a favorable change. I watched for side effects but couldn't see any. It seemed strange not to react with tears or extreme highs and lows in my emotions.

I was part of a small group that met weekly in Destin, Florida. A friend approached me with a tiny ornament the size of a bouillon cube. Wrapped in red foil and tied with thin gold string, it looked like a miniature gift. Placing it in my hand, she said, "I felt the Lord wanted you to have this."

Seventeen years later, I still use a plastic pill organizer that holds my medication. The small ornament is also there to remind me of God's gift to manage bipolar depression. There have been several times over the years when I've questioned if I need the medication. I feel so balanced and healthy. I no longer need to go for a ride in the car to release my tears.

But I'm reminded that those kinds of thoughts are part of the bipolar condition. It's not an indication to stop taking the pills, but rather to be thankful that they are working to keep me steady and stable. I have been in remission since 2004.

When we shared our story with the pastor of our church, he accused me of being mentally ill, and we were excluded from certain aspects of service in the church. Sadly, this led to our son Kris distancing from the youth group that had been so meaningful to him. It took me many years to truly forgive the pastor and those in the church body who failed to support us.

Consequently, we searched for a new church home in many locations and denominations, never really discovering where we fit. Until…God answered our prayer in His time.

"Gifts"

Words/music: Jeanie Connell, February 1993

Thank You, Jesus, thank You for the tears,
Such a funny present I overlooked for years.
Thank You, Jesus, thank You for the shame,
I once thought it was ugly, but that's before You came.

Thank You, Jesus, thank You for the pain.
I've learned that, with rainbows, they follow rain.
Thank You, Jesus, thank You mostly for Your love.
It's like the sky, unending, it covers from above.

Gifts, gifts, gifts! **We think we know the ones we want.**
Gifts, gifts, gifts, I like the ones my neighbor got.
Gifts, gifts, gifts, I never thought I wanted tears,
Gifts, gifts, gifts, it's taken me so many years . . .

For me to say, "Thank You, Jesus, thank You, You had Your way.
Not the way I planned it—what can I say?
Thank You, Jesus, thank You mostly for today.
With the gifts You gave me, **You taught me how to pray.**

Thank You…thank You…Jesus.

Listen to this song at jeanieconnell.org/music.

Chapter 25
ONE FLESH

Kris graduated from high school in 2007. The week he left for college, I began work on a new recording. Meeting my producer in the local music shop, he offered to listen to a demo of my latest songs. My music proved a great focus as I faced an empty nest.

The Y in this touristy beach town never launched. No longer employed by the YMCA after nearly thirty years, Michael was offered a source of income by a generous friend and his company, which allowed us to pay our bills until Michael's retirement became official. This gesture led to an invitation for Michael to teach and coach basketball at Destin Christian Academy.

I never could have dreamed this would be the state where we would live the longest. During those Florida years, I wrote poems in blank journals and shared them with friends, never imagining they would be published in my 2009 book, *God's Heartstrings—I Call His Name.*[1]

As our marriage grew stronger, we renewed our vows in 2008, on our thirty-seventh wedding anniversary. I wrote a song called "One Flesh" to reflect our relationship.

Kyle, one of the pastors at a church in Georgia, made the renewing of our vows ceremony official. All three of our children joined us, as well as Kyle's fiancée and Libby's future husband.

No more was the voice in my head saying, *Promise You Won't Remember*. I now had my own mantra: *I Call His Name*, which is also the name of one of my CDs.

That same year, Kyle and Rebecca married. In November of 2012, Libby eloped with Erik in Las Vegas. Our youngest son, Kris, would marry his beautiful bride, Teona, in 2014.

"One Flesh"

Words/music: Jeanie Connell, June 2008

He is an athlete, I'm a musician.
My choice is seafood, he prefers steak.
He loves adventure, I favor Disney.
Somehow, we share in the choices we make.

CHORUS: And you won't know him if you don't know me.
'Cause I am a part of his personality.
And you won't know me if you don't know him,
You'll only know part, and that part will be dim.

He is a coach and I'm a songwriter.
He is a man who works with a plan.
I am impulsive, that's just my nature.
If it's spontaneous, I'll lend a hand.

CHORUS

He is a strong man and not much for crying.
I have a strong will, but wealthy with tears.
We've learned what one has belongs to the other.
Introvert, extrovert, down through the years.

CHORUS

Here is the last verse, we have a Savior.

Though we are different, here we agree.

Two make a couple, we become one flesh.

Only in Christ we're a chord of three.

*And you won't know **Him** if you cannot see that He formed your life and your personality.*

It's only in Him that we stand to be a marriage today, and a chord of three.[2]

Chapter 26
IN THE BLINK OF AN EYE

The church we attended for most of our sixteen years in Florida, Eastgate Christian Fellowship, provided a place where you could feel accepted for who you were. We worshiped Jesus led by a band who were sometimes barefoot. Surfboards hung from the walls, and our pastor taught from the Bible, one book, one chapter, and one verse at a time.

In 2014, one brave married mother of three shared her story of child sexual abuse. She invited other women to join her in a healing journey using Dan Allender's book, *The Wounded Heart: Hope for Adult Victims* (1995). Thank you, Misti! This small group proved life-changing for each of us.

Another close friend at Eastgate, brave in many ways, lost her battle with cancer, leaving behind three little girls and her husband. Her bravery served as an example to each of us. *I love you, Irene Paige! Thank you for suggesting the title for this book and for your listening ear. I will never forget you or your amazing smile!*

In October 2018, Hurricane Michael ripped through Panama City, Florida, and surrounding areas, leaving thousands homeless or at least roofless. The most damaging storm in the

Panhandle's history left many residents with painful memories from the terrifying event.

A year later, in 2019, many families were still trying to cope with ruined businesses and a city that remained unrecognizable. Miles of trees either wiped out completely or broken off as though a chainsaw had sliced them in half.

We were grateful to have our roof replaced and our damages repaired. In April, Michael and I, rather impulsively, decided to put our house on the market. Nine days later, it sold before we could discuss where we would relocate.

You know what we did…we prayed.

On the phone with my *forever friend* Meg, who still lived outside of Nashville, she said excitedly, "You must come to Franklin, Tennessee! Haven't you heard that *everyone* is moving here?" She followed her enthusiastic invitation by texting the addresses of several apartment complexes in the area.

All our kids were thrilled, and Libby and Erik helped us downsize from our three-bedroom home to a one-bedroom apartment. During the following month, we sold or gave away everything that wouldn't fit in our two compact cars. Adding to the experience were the shingles on my entire right side and the medication to keep the pain under control.

We came sight unseen and ended up next to the Tennessee hills, where the seasons change four times a year, and Michael works part time at the golf course, while I write.

I wrote the following essay to be critiqued by my *Word Weavers* group that meets monthly to encourage writers working in any genre. First becoming a member in Destin, Florida, I transferred to the group in Nashville, and later found my tribe in Shelbyville, Tennessee.

"Puzzle Pieces"
December 9, 2019

When I entered my first psychiatric hospital in 1986 with Post-Traumatic Stress Disorder, I imagined watching puzzle pieces dropping down on a table in front of me. Looking at them, I couldn't fit them together. Exhausted after a week of flashbacks, discouragement settled in my mind and heart. Darkness surrounded me. So many years I had prayed asking God to make me whole, but the scattered puzzle pieces revealed my brokenness.

I like puzzles, although I never remember putting one together from beginning to end. This week, I bought a puzzle that displays the twenty-five days of December through Christmas Day. Happiness wrapped around me like a blanket as I purchased my puzzle. Connecting some pieces, I found myself thinking about the mental hospital years ago and wanting to be whole. *God, are You trying to show me something?*

Putting the outer edges together formed the border around the daily events and activities leading up to Christmas—and reminding me of the boundaries I had to develop years ago. With the joy of a child mastering a new skill, I connected different pieces. Memories emerged from my past when I sought help through counseling and prayer.

As I worked on the interlocking pieces, the parallels between this activity and my work through therapy continued to emerge. Occasionally, the puzzle became tedious as I tried relentlessly to make the pieces fit. At times, I had to step back and take a break. Counseling had been the same. *Why couldn't I make the process go faster?*

Anyone seeing the disconnected pieces on the table would only have considered them an engaging pastime. But, between me and God, they became so much more. He partnered with me to provide a visual tool that put my past in perspective.

Typical of many puzzles, the beginning went slowly. Eventually, when I began seeing the picture emerge, it compared to riding a bicycle downhill. What fun!

The purpose of any puzzle is to join each piece and make the picture complete. What a reminder of my persistence in counseling when early on the flashbacks didn't make sense and the memories were like missing pieces.

Working my Christmas project, I felt my heart suddenly sink. There were five lost pieces. *How could I have let this happen? I have no one to blame but myself.* Reminding me of counseling thirty years prior, I found a way to blame myself for anything I couldn't understand.

I found four of the missing pieces under the table and my hope was restored. With excitement I secured them together and reached for my phone to take a snapshot. That's when I saw the tiny space on the edge without a connecting piece.

A puzzle we completed during Christmas, 2020

I turned over all the furniture cushions, lay on the floor to scan the entire room at floor level, and eventually gave up my search, deciding I could live with a puzzle missing only one piece. I wondered, *God, what would You like me to learn from this experience? Will there always be a missing piece in our lives? Can I be satisfied when I'm less than whole?*

Then, directly in front of me on the kitchen floor, lay the missing piece! Mystery solved. I imagined God smiled, saying, *Jeanie, I wanted you to see that you once were lost and now are found. Remember, I am the One who made you whole.*

With the puzzle complete, I decided to give it away as a gift to my friend Laurel for her birthday.

Packing it carefully in the original box, I thought of one more analogy. When we become whole, we are ready to pass on to others the love and comfort we have received from God. "Father of compassion and God of all comfort, who comforts us in all our troubles, so that we can comfort those in any trouble with the comfort we ourselves receive from God" (2 Corinthians 1:3–4).

Writing my memoir without childhood memories felt like being invisible. I wanted to deny that putting my thoughts and ideas on paper provided a type of therapy, when in truth that's what it has done. I feared that I might lose my memories, so I kept replaying them in my mind. Slowly, in the writing of my story, it began to feel safe to let the memories move from my mind to the page. To imagine that they might bring hope or help to someone else would be like giving away my puzzle as a gift, because all we really give to others is exactly who we are.

Our lives are His story. If for any reason you have been

afraid to trust Him, I pray you will make that decision today because everything can change…in the blink of an eye.

"In the Blink of an Eye"

Words/music: Jeanie Connell, October 30, 2018

In the blink of an eye, I'll see Your face,
In the moment You choose I'll know Your grace,
In the plan for my life — to me unknown,
May I glorify You and You alone!

CHORUS: In the blink of an eye, in the rush of the wind,
In the depths of a flood or the prison of sin,
In the darkest of night when we long for the day,
May we rest in Your love and learn to pray!

When I sing of Your name — I see Your face,
When I'm broken or scared, I know Your grace,
When I wonder what plans You have for me,
I am blessed when I'm found on bended knee.

CHORUS

All of the treasure's life can hold
Never compare to what You've told
Me in Your Word. I trust Your way.
Help me to live for You this day!

Listen to this song at jeanieconnell.org/music.

Chapter 27
I CALL YOU DAUGHTER

Yesterday, September 7, 2021, I had an appointment for healing prayer session at the church where I attend. Eager to be able to use this kind of approach myself, I met with a team of three. (I am not using their real names.) The office had a cozy feel. We began with listening prayer. Quiet. Each attentive to the inside voice of the Holy Spirit. Alex (who led), Jenny, and Mandy took notes, and gave me handwritten scriptures they had prayed for me before the session.

I spoke what came into my mind or followed *Repeat-After-Me Prayers*. Alex explained that *repeat-after-me-prayers* are not to force rote repetition but to help someone find words to say what they mean, or need to say, to unleash the power of their heartfelt feelings, and to make a declaration to change things in the spirit. They just "prime the pump" and often lead to the person finding their own words to declare new things in new ways.

In listening, I heard that I was safe. Alex showed me where he had just written that down. He asked if I wanted to share anything.

Immediately, I thought of a song by Christy Nockels, "Keep the Light On." I first heard her sing the lullaby in October 2018, and every time I listened over three years, I cried. Not happy tears, but as though pain were oozing out from somewhere inside of me. It takes a lot for me to cry, but I could always count on Christy's song to trigger my emotions.

I brought up the song on my phone and played it for the prayer team. I didn't cry. I wept. I sobbed. Cries of grief escaped from the deepest part of me. My body shook and tears fell faster than Kleenex could catch them. The song played on.

As the song concluded, my head throbbed. For someone who finds it difficult to cry, my tears over the next two hours made up for the past years of drought.

Alex helped unpack my strong reaction to the song by asking questions. He identified an unhealthy "soul tie" (a relationship that, purposefully or not, improperly controls a person) with Dr. Ross and Jill. He asked if I could pray after him. Yes. Speaking sentence after sentence out loud, the words became my own and untangled the cords of dependency that had grown over the years.

Alex prayed, "Jesus, what does the little one need?"

Me: (tearfully) "When I draw near to Abba Father, Dr. Ross and Jill show up. If they go, what will fill their place in my heart?"

As Alex asked what I saw, I said, "My children and my grands. Abba Father, will You be there to help fill the empty place?"

Alex, "Ask the little girl if it's enough to have these with you to feel safe."

"Yes!" I heard and said.

I also declared: "Dr. Ross, and Jill, thank you for helping me, but you created a heart-condition, and I became dependent on you. I didn't know how to escape. Today I declare my freedom. I renounce my soul ties. I sever the relationship. Abba, cleanse my mind. I break the entanglement. I speak clearly what I need."

Alex spoke to the little girl inside me, "Little one, you are beloved, safe, free to speak, sing, and be who you are." His words were soothing. Truth entering straight to my heart.

I declared: "Jesus, You, are my big brother. (I had always wanted one.) When I go to sleep would it be okay if You were with me?"

"Jesus says He is there. Thank You Jesus!"

Being led in a declaration, I said: "I now speak to every spirit who does not bow to Jesus Christ and who took advantage of me. I command you now to shut your mouths and go to the feet of Jesus. I break every agreement, renounce lies I believed, tear down every stronghold and false way of the enemy. I have the mind of Christ. My Big Brother is with me and in me. He is with the little one and she is strong. She is a daddy's girl. I close the door on Jill and Dr. Ross." (With my eyes still closed I see the counseling offices where I spent seven years. The door is closed. Closed forever.)

Alex helps again with another repeat-after-me prayer:

"Jesus, cleanse my mind. I'm not asking You to change the memories, but to show me the truth. I choose to take back everything stolen from me because I am a strong child of the King. In the name of Jesus, my Lord."

We ask Jesus to show me if there is anything else I need to give Him today.

Clearly, I hear, "Anger. It's an awful gift to give you Jesus, but I don't want it anymore."

I ask Abba Father where I learned to be angry.

"My mom."

Alex suggests we speak directly to Mom.

"Mom, I'm sorry for all you went through because of your dad. I'm sorry no one told you about bipolar or helped you feel better. I am sorry you couldn't love yourself. I am glad you loved Jesus. Mom, you owed me gentleness and nurture, but you couldn't give it to me because of your dad. Today I forgive you for not being gentle or nurturing and for teaching us that we couldn't trust you. I forgive you for not showing us a healthy way to express our emotions.

Spirit of anger, leave me now and any spirit that came with you. I renounce my anger. Spirit of anger, I break my relationship with you. Replace it with the fruit of the spirit: peace, patience, and gentleness."

Following Alex, I declare: "I am in a family that does not need to use rage and anger to cover pain. I give it all to you, Abba Father. What else do I need to give You?"

"Judgment. I know your Word says, 'Judge not or you will be judged.'"

"I renounce and repent of judging others. I break the spirit of judgment. I renounce the lie that I can judge because I am so smart. I humble myself as your child, Abba, and I give it all to You. Thank You for your forgiveness and understanding. Thank You Jesus for taking away my shortcomings."

Being led to declare again, I say: "I am a new creation. I am a new person, a daughter of the King. I say to the little one, 'We don't have to judge. We can bless.' I am a princess, and I can ask the best for others. I give all judgment to You; Father God and I claim my identity back as a child of God."

As I speak these words they fall like gentle rain on thirsty ground. They are changing me, transforming me inside. I believe Abba Father specifically chose the words for me. To heal me and set me free.

I declared: "My last years will be more powerful than anything Satan has ever seen. I am free and destined to the throne room. I don't judge but invite others to the throne room."

I paused for a moment and added: "That is my story and I'm sticking with it!" (The prayer team laughed, and the little girl felt brave.)

One last time Alex asked the question, "Abba Father, is there anything else You want to show Jeanie?"

The words stuck in my throat. It didn't seem important enough to mention. I felt so undeserving that three people who hardly knew me would take the time to listen and pray for me. Then, out popped the words. "God gives me songs, and I used to sing them without caring what people thought. It's different now. I am so grateful for the songs Father gives me, but I am embarrassed to sing them. It makes me different."

Alex responded, "Singing is one of the highest expressions of praise to the Lord. Even David danced before the Lord, not caring what people thought. We are told to sing a new song to the Lord."

I then follow Alex in prayer: "Abba Father, you have searched me to the very depths of who I am. My songs come from the deepest part of me. They cleanse and sanctify me. I thank You for the songs! I have an audience of One, and I hear You clapping. I say, 'Yes, the little girl gets to sing!' Satan, you have no part in this. You are not in the Kingdom."

I added, "DKB."

Alex asks, "Doing Kingdom Business?"

I nod my head yes. And Alex responds, "Yes, we are Doing Kingdom Business! You get an A."

I smile with the little girl.

Alex admits that he has received several songs of praise. The little girl asks if he would sing one.

As I listen to his strong voice sing over me, I felt overwhelmed by Abba's love. He alone knew I had waited a lifetime to hear someone sing over me with Father's love.

Alex says, "Maybe we need to ask Father what songs He wants to sing over us."

Driving home after prayer, I put Christy Nockels recording in my CD player. I shed no tears! My joy served as a confirmation of the freedom that had taken place.

September 7, 2021, after my prayer ministry time, Abba sang a new song over me, *I Call You Daughter.* Until today, I never recognized the songs Abba Father sang over me as His child.

Full circle—finally complete. A book twenty-six years in the writing. From chapter one through the epilogue. My prayer is a familiar verse:

"My sheep listen to my voice; I know them, and they follow me. I give them eternal life, and they shall never perish; no one can snatch them out of my hand" (John 10:27–28).

"I Call You Daughter"

Words/music: Jeanie Connell, September 8, 2021

I call you daughter. I call you little one.
You are my princess, beloved, my child.
You have always been Daddy's girl.
I designed your hair with its curl.
I have watched you spin, dance, and twirl in front of Me.

When you feel alone or afraid,
Run into My arms, you'll be safe.
I will draw you close, singing over you
I will be your strength!

Listen to this song at jeanieconnell.org/music.

Chapter 28
MEMORY

October 21, 2021

Waking up after a good night's sleep, my first conscious thought was a memory. My next thought: *Did I include this memory in my book?* I knew I hadn't because it was covered in shame and fear. *What would people think of me if they read it? How could my children understand? God, the book goes to print in weeks! Why now? I prayed Deuteronomy 29:29 about things in secret. Why are You revealing this now?*

Posing that question to my friend Mimi, she responded: "Jeanie, God knew exactly when to give the memory to you. After all, it's His story."

The memory is represented by one word: it acts as a trigger.

The definition of trigger in mental health terms is as follows:

A trigger is something that significantly affects our emotional state of mind. It causes extreme distress and overwhelms us. A trigger impacts our ability to remain in the present moment and seems to transport us to the past event. It can bring up specific thoughts patterns and even influence our behavior with feelings of fear, shame, or guilt.[1]

The isolated memory I'm trying not to talk about continues to bring shame every time I get a glimpse of it. All through the years, I have wanted memories, but this is one I wish I didn't have. *Why does it stay alive in my memory when it brings such shame?* I am alone in the memory.

Around the same time that I began having this memory, I was having lunch with my friend Erika. I told her about a counseling session I had with Jill more than thirty years ago when I tried to speak a certain word out loud. "I made Jill promise that once I said the word, she would not repeat it or ask me about it."

I closed my eyes tight so she couldn't see the little girl. For the first time I could remember, I said the word out loud. I was like a turtle poking it's head out for only seconds, then quickly hiding back in its shell. Jill kept her promise. No discussion. Ever.

I said the word diaper.

Today, with Erika, I didn't feel brave enough to say the word out loud, so I wrote the word on a piece of paper. I reached in my purse for a pen and looked for something to write on. I grabbed the devotional *Our Daily Bread* and ripped out a page from September. I wrote the word *diaper* and handed it to Erika. She asked me how old I was in the memory.

"I know I was a child. Maybe ten. I can't remember any

clues to indicate my age," I said. I see every detail: myself, my surroundings, and remember my feelings. The feeling of shame is intense, powerful, and all encompassing. I'm in a dark, hidden place. *Never tell.*

In attempting to help me process this memory, she used the word infantile something. Erika responded gently. She is a therapist and thinks professionally.

I looked up *infantile amnesia* which describes the loss of early memories from three years old to ten resulting from an early sexual experience. It felt like a validation of my story.

Greatly conflicted about what Abba Father wanted me to do with the memory, I felt strangely peaceful about sharing it with Erika. She handed me back the devotion page where I'd written the word diaper, and we said our goodbyes.

PLEASE, PLEASE JESUS, HELP ME UNDERSTAND.

My sleep that night was interrupted, and I felt the Lord calling me to sit with Him in my prayer room. Sitting in my chair, which feels like Abba Father's lap, I poured out my heart. My fears caused me to tremble at times, the tears came hard and then subsided. This single memory from my youth evoked such shame. How could a word that I was not able to speak, be printed in my book for everyone to see? My thoughts were racing faster than I could process them. *In the morning should I call a therapist or sign up for another prayer session? How do I deal with this newly uncovered information?*

I heard the Lord say, "In the morning, call your sister."

By five a.m., I returned to bed and asked Michael to pray for me. His words were full of truth, reminding me of Jesus love, the healing He had given me, and of His constant care. I slept.

In my prayer room a few hours later, on October 22, 2021, I read Isaiah 41:13 NIV "For I am the Lord, your God, who takes hold of your right hand and says to you, do not fear; I will help you."

Abba Father spoke to me again with Psalm 62:8: "Trust in Him at all times, you people; pour out your hearts to Him, for God is our refuge." What a perfect description of the previous night in my prayer room.

Kathy returned my call. I shared the memory that had remained hidden all our lives. She shared some of her own personal memories of our grandfather with me. Her voice held compassion and understanding. I had something else to share with her. I found the devotional page in my purse where I had written the word diaper and began to read the *Our Daily Bread* printed devotion: "My family remembers my **grandpa**." I sat staring at the words in unbelief! The remainder of the words on the page were about prayer. "Pray continually, give thanks in all circumstances; for this is God's will for you in Christ Jesus" (1 Thessalonians 5:18). I knew beyond a shadow of a doubt that my Jesus was showing me the way. Being reassured of His powerful love, strong enough to demolish shame, God took the lead. He took me by the hand, reminding me of the following verse: "Yet I am always with you; You hold me by my right hand. You guide me with Your counsel, and afterward You will take me into glory" (Psalm 73:23–24).

This one word, one memory, was one small piece of the puzzle of my life. Look at the Christmas puzzle with the missing piece. Just one small piece on the edge, was enough to convince me I couldn't be whole. The enemy wanted me to believe that the missing piece defined me.

By October 25, 2021, three days later, I am certain that the memory is God's gift to me. A gift that will help others venture into wholeness unafraid. Like me, they will be running into the arms of Abba Father to pour out their hearts to Him and receive refuge.

One memory linked to a million moments of shame and fear.

At age ten, I went into our bathroom and peed standing up at the toilet. Then I got a bath towel and used it as a diaper. *I'm sick. I'm disgusting. I'm shameful. I want to feel the good feeling in my lower body. No one knows. I tell no one. Ever. How could I? Why would I?*

Throughout my life if I even heard the word "diaper," fear, panic, and shame erupt. I had been unable to say that word.

The missing piece was that my grandfather used to shame me by telling me I needed a diaper. He used sick, shaming words as he touched my small, undeveloped breasts. He made me feel like I wanted it because it gave me a "good feeling" as he manipulated me. Afterwards, I entered a dark place. I didn't think Jesus was there. I heard about Jesus in church and Sunday school, but I hadn't met Him.

As an adult, I would wake up with ugly dreams of someone touching me as a small child. I thought that made *me* ugly for even having those thoughts in my mind. I never realized they came from isolated moments, repressed memories with my grandfather.

Grandfather did perverted things, accountable to no one, both at the creek near our house and in his private basement. Following the shame and regret, my body remembered the "good feeling" that followed. Seeking to repeat it, partial pieces of memory returned during intimate moments in our marriage. The flashbacks made sense for the first time! The early childhood memories I thought I wanted became the very core of my shame.

As an adult, I once attended a baby shower for a friend, and one of the games was to diaper yourself with toilet paper. My anxiety was off-the-charts, and it felt like people could see the shame hiding inside of me. I had to leave. I determined I would never let myself be put in that position again. It wasn't a game to me. It was a form of torture.

Writing this chapter may possibly be one of the most difficult things I have ever done.

When I first began asking Abba Father if He wanted me to include the memory in my book, I heard Him say, "You don't *have to* put it in the book." I pondered, *Why didn't God say, don't include it in your story?*

I was reminded of my first counselor in Shelby, Ohio. When I saw Debi for anorexia, she would end every appointment by saying, "Jeanie, you don't *have to* eat when you go home." I relaxed and didn't feel pressure. I would go home and eat without feelings of fear.

Just knowing I didn't have to include the shameful memory in my book, allowed me to relax and let go of the fear. I trusted God, day by day, that He would show me the way and reveal His plan and purpose.

It turned out that as difficult as writing the details was, it became equally difficult to say them out loud.

When I told Michael the trigger word connected to my memory in the bathroom as a ten-year-old, he responded, "Jeanie, you told me about the word diaper thirty years ago. You were extremely emotional when you told me, and you seemed out of control. Seeing you that distraught, I assumed you were talking to Jill about it."

Michael continued, "Babe, if you only put the one-word trigger in the book, your readers will not understand what actually took place. It leaves me confused myself."

Shocked that I had actually shared the word so many years ago when I was seeing Jill, I now asked if I could share my recent memory.

"Babe, if you are ready to tell me, I'm ready to listen," Michael reassured me.

After sharing the missing puzzle pieces when I was a ten-year-old, he responded, "Honey, this needs to be in your book.

Your readers will see the greater miracle God has done in your life."

That was the answer I had been searching for. No turning back.

Michael and Jeanie (left and right): Fall 1970, Millburn, New Jersey, engaged; June 26, 2021: 50ᵗʰ Wedding Anniversary in Las Vegas

My *memory* wasn't told to a therapist or psychiatrist or my sister or even a close friend. I felt safe enough to share with my husband of fifty years.

The same day I received an email from my editor/publisher asking for my finished manuscript by October 30. God's timing leaves me in awe.

As I finished writing, my phone rang, and I answered: "Hey Cherie!"

"Um, no, this is Jeanie," responding to my friend Jan on the other end.

"Oh, I'm sorry I called you by mistake, Jeanie! Well, wait," Jan continued, "Maybe it wasn't a mistake."

Jan Powell is an editor I met during a Christian Writers retreat in 2020. She knew I was writing a memoir that included child sexual abuse. We hadn't spoken for months, and she called a wrong number that just happened to be me.

Jan explained that her friend would be opening her Christian counseling practice and asked Jan if she knew of any authors who had written about their personal experience with child sexual abuse.

Jan asked about my launch date for this book and then agreed to purchase three copies! I had made my first book sale, before the book was available for purchase!

I refer to this type of situation as *confirmation* from the Lord! It was His way of saying, "You are on the right track."

When I think of His confirmation, I think of the following verse: "Whether you turn to the right or to the left, your ears will hear a voice behind you saying, 'This is the way; walk in it" (Isaiah 30:21). When it came to what to include in my book—just as in my life, He has always guided me. I'm so grateful. I am also grateful for the way He transformed me, preserved me from harm, and how He is now using my pain to encourage others struggling with depression, eating disorders, anxiety, low self-esteem, and fragmented personality. He has made me a butterfly for those who He puts in my path.

May He receive the glory for His healing in my life and use this story to touch the lives of others.

A LETTER FROM
ABBA FATHER

Because God's words are eternal and outweigh my words, I wanted to end this book with a letter that He downloaded to me as I thought about you—the readers of this book. May it bring you as much comfort and peace as it gave me when I received it from Him.

Dear Beloved,

I have known, before Jeanie wrote this book, that you would read it. I know you inside and out and love you beyond your imaginings (Psalm 139:1). I know your broken places, and if you allow Me, I will heal them. I hold all the memories you can't recall, as well as the ones you would like to forget. You can trust Me with your heart.

"Remember the former things, those of long ago; I am God, and there is no other; I am God, and there is none like Me" (Isaiah 46:9).

Just as there is no God like Me, there is no Father like me. The most loving father on earth will not compare with the love I have for you. I am the father you have always wanted.

I am your provider and will take care of all your needs (Matthew 6:31–33).

I delight in you and sing over you (Zephaniah 3:17.) I gave up everything I loved so I could gain your love (Romans 8:32). Nothing will ever separate you from My love (Romans 8:38–39). If you receive the gift of My Son Jesus, you receive Me (1 John 2:23).

I'm waiting for you. I will never let you go because My love is everlasting (Jeremiah 31:3).

You may be grown, but you are still My child. Will you allow Me to hold you and comfort you and encourage you to be all I have planned for you to be? (2 Thessalonians 2:16–17) I have always loved you. I always will love you…

Love,

Abba, Your Father and Almighty God

"I am the way, the truth and the life" (John 14:6).

EPILOGUE

The milestones in my life were brought about through prayer. Jesus keeps His promises. When He says He will never leave us or forsake us we can believe Him. Today holds more joy than I ever dreamed possible. I still struggle at times with fear of rejection. I still sometimes expect more of myself than I can give and expect more of others than they are able to give.

Today, one of my greatest joys is being a member of a church where I can serve. I have gone through training to minister on our prayer team. And in the coming months, I will meet with a small group of women to read and discuss the questions in this book. I consider that a great honor and privilege.

C.J. and I are no longer two separate personalities. I am grateful to know and love that part of myself. She no longer makes my decisions, but she does make herself known. Her presence is a reminder to let my heavenly Father sing over her, and for me not to take life too seriously.

Living with depression for any length of time and then experiencing freedom is hard to describe. In place of tears, I can laugh with family and friends. Even the weather makes me glad I'm alive. My time with Jesus, reading His Word, is my favorite part of the day.

Listening is a powerful tool to healing our hearts. That's what we experience if we go see a good therapist. He or she can never take the place of our friends. I caution you, though, from my experience. Pay attention to your gut feelings: Are you being true to yourself? Are you trying to please them? Are you becoming dependent on your relationship with him or her?

Regarding medication, depression of any type is a treatable condition. Don't be afraid to search for the right prescription and take it consistently. Pray and let God lead you in that decision.

I hope God's plan for my future will include recording a Christmas CD of original songs and publishing a children's book I wrote in 2011, *Before You Were Born.*

I love meeting people, seeing how God connects His puzzle pieces. I would love to hear your story. Connect with me at Jeanieconnell.org

DISCUSSION QUESTIONS FOR SUPPORT GROUPS

Guidelines:

1) There are no wrong answers.
2) What is said in the group stays within the group.
3) Use encouraging words and positive comments only.

Chapter 1—The Fast

1) Have you ever felt God called you to fast? What were the circumstances?
2) If you attend church, do they practice fasting and prayer?
3) Find one verse in the Bible that mentions fasting.
4) Can you identify a time in your life when things took a turn for the better? Describe what happened.

Chapter 2—Shine Through Me

1) How would you personally define or describe deliverance?
2) Do you believe in demons?

3) Take turns speaking Isaiah 43:1 over each person in your group, using his or her given name.

4) Have you experienced brokenness in your life that led you to therapy, a pastor, or a friend?

Chapter 3—Promise You Won't Remember

1) Are you a person who remembers your past?

2) How does the quote, "You don't know what you don't know," apply to your life?

3) Is there a difficult truth you have discovered as an adult?

4) Do you have a favorite memory? If so, write about it or share it. It can be from any age.

Chapter 4—Black and White

1) How would you define "black and white thinking?"

2) If you could go to a trusted Christian counselor at no cost, every week for two months, what subject would you talk about?

3) Where are you in the birth order of your original family? (First born, middle, youngest.) Discuss how your birth order affected your life.

Chapter 5—Jesus, Do Ya Ever Call Me "Baby"?

1) If you could choose a nickname, what would it be? Would you be willing to answer to that title in your group?

2) Are you familiar with the term "inner child?" If so, what does the term mean to you?

3) Have you had words spoken over you that still *sting?* (Or any that still bring joy?)

Chapter 6—Flashbacks

1) Do you have a "life verse"—a scripture that is like your anchor in the storm? If you are unfamiliar with that term or do not have such a verse, ask your heavenly Father for one today. Then work to memorize it.

2) Have you ever been hospitalized for any reason and felt afraid?

3) Do you think mental illness carries a stigma?

Chapter 7—Psychiatrist Number Two

1) *Dr. Ross never filled silences with words unless they were necessary.* Is that statement like the words in the following verse: "My dear brothers and sisters, take note of this; everyone should be quick to listen, slow to speak, and slow to become angry" (James 1:19)?

2) Are children quick to listen, slow to speak, and slow to become angry? How can we as adults become more patient?

Chapter 8—Learning the Hard Way

1) Is your appearance the first thing you want others to notice about you? (If yes, why?)

2) Can you share a circumstance when you regretted your behavior?

3) Do you recall an instance when you were trying to gain attention? If so, what happened?

Chapter 9—Was I Sexually Abused?

1) Can you remember placing your hope in someone and being disappointed? If so, have you processed the hurt and forgave your perpetrator?

2) What answer would you give if someone asked you how to make a memory?

3) Have you ever felt depression or despondency that led you to a dangerous action?

Chapter 10—Always in a Hurry

1) How would you describe your positive or negative experience with church?

2) Is medication something you would welcome or oppose?

3) Have you ever responded to someone's *I love you* by repeating it back, knowing it didn't have the same meaning for them as it did for you?

Chapter 11—Behind a Wall

1) What have you found to be your healthiest method of getting rid of anger?

2) Did you grow up in a family where it was safe (natural) to talk about your feelings? Talk about what growing up was like for you and how you wish it might have been different. Then describe how you might foster more open communication moving forward.

3) What is your definition of the word anger?

Chapter 12—One Step at a Time

1) What comes to mind when you think of "weathering a storm" in a marriage or close relationship?

2) When you read Jill's invitation to be *the child they never had*, describe your initial reaction.

3) Have you ever daydreamed about having a different parent or having a loving brother or sister?

4) What does Ephesians 4:26, "In your anger do not sin. Do not let the sun go down while you are still angry," mean to you?

Chapter 13—Regrets

1) Can you remember a time when you felt helpless? Frightened? Guilty? Ashamed? (Choose one and describe the situation.)

2) Have you ever been to a retreat? Can you describe what your ideal retreat would look like? (Where is it? Who's there? What is the theme? Who is leading worship?)

Chapter 14—Only Once

1) If you could know someone more intimately, who would it be? (Friend, loved one, stranger, movie star?)
2) Has there been anyone in your life that you've lost through death, divorce, or distance? (Can you share?)
3) Have you ever owned a favorite doll, stuffed animal, or security blanket? (Identify.)

Chapter 15—Mom

1) How would you rate your mom on a scale of one to ten? (Honestly, without guilt.)
2) Who is the most difficult person you've ever had to confront?
3) Have you ever felt you were responsible for disappointing one of your parents?

Chapter 16—Unexpected Surprise

1) What's the most unusual gift anyone has ever given you?
2) If you could choose one fruit of the spirit from Galatians 5:22–23: "love, joy, peace, patience, kindness, goodness, faithfulness, gentleness, self-control,"which would you choose and why?

3) Do you have any brothers or sisters who show a family resemblance to you? If so, what do you appreciate about that sibling?

Chapter 17—Once upon a Time

1) When you have a plan or idea in place, is it difficult to encounter a roadblock? How do you respond?

2) Do you have unrealistic expectations? (For people or circumstances?) If so, what can you do to help rectify them?

3) 1 Corinthians 2:9 says: "What no eye has seen, what no ear has heard, and what no human mind has conceived—the things God has prepared for those who love Him." Does this scripture help you to trust God with your expectations?

Chapter 18—Time to Say Goodbye

1) Read Jeremiah 29:11 and discuss whether you believe God has a great plan for you.

2) If your life was a book, would it be a drama, a comedy, or a fairytale?

3) How does God speak to you?

4) Can you think of a time you felt unprepared to face tragedy or pain? What happened?

Chapter 19—Let It Go

1) How would you define codependency? Have you personally experienced this, or do you know someone who has?

2) What or who is the hardest thing you have had to let go of in your life?

3) Have you ever been guilty of stalking someone?

Chapter 20—New Beginnings

1) What comes to mind when you hear the word "boundaries?"

2) Can you think of a time when you found it difficult to say, "I'm sorry?"

3) What is your response to Jorge Luis Borges's poem about saying goodbye?

4) Which phrase best describes you today?

- Ready for a new beginning

- Recently experienced a new beginning

- Resisting a new beginning

Chapter 21—Little Girl

1) Which of the seven statements from *I Can Grow Up* can you relate to the most?

"Other people are as special as me."

"Feelings are something God understands."

"Angry feelings don't have to hurt other people."

"I can like myself when I make mistakes."

"I can change me; I cannot change other people."

"Safe is something very important that everyone needs to feel."

"With enough loving, I can grow up."

2) Have you ever had a positive or negative experience with counseling?

3) What is the best birthday gift you have ever received?

Chapter 22—Butterfly

1) Would you rather pray out loud, sing out loud, or read out loud? Or would you rather do none of the above? Why or why not?

2) Would you prefer to work in a garden, read a book, or bake a cake in your free time?

3) What would you throw into a bonfire if given the chance?

Chapter 23—Illusion

1) What is a "last" that you remember? (Was it happy or sad?)

2) When was the last time you prayed with your husband, partner, or friend, while holding hands?

3) Have you ever been in a relationship that was one-sided? (One person needed you and depended on you to meet their needs?) If so, how did you feel? What can you do about a one-sided relationship?

Chapter 24—Gifts

1) Have you ever been given a gift that didn't seem like a gift at the time?

2) What's your favorite book or movie? (Why?)

3) Have you thanked God lately for your tears, your pain, or your trials?

Chapter 25—One Flesh

1) Have you ever written in a journal?

2) Do you prefer the beach to the mountains? Describe why.

3) Do you know where the term "one flesh" originated? If so, please share.

4) Read and reflect on Jesus' words in Mark 10:6–9: "But at the beginning of creation God made them male and female. For this reason, a man will leave his father and mother and be united to his wife, and the two will become one flesh. So, they are no longer two, but one flesh. Therefore, what God has joined together, let no one separate."

Chapter 26—Blink of an Eye

1) Have you ever lived through a tornado, hurricane, or flood? Describe what happened.

2) Can you remember putting together a puzzle? Have a member of your group bring a puzzle to work on together and describe the experience. Leave out a middle piece. What does it represent?

3) 2 Corinthians 1:34 says: "God of all comfort...who comforts you *so that* you can comfort others...with the comfort you have received." Describe the comfort you received and are now able to pass on to someone in need.

Chapter 27—I Call You Daughter

1) Have you been set free? John 8:36 says: "Then you will know the truth, and the truth will set you free."

2) Do you feel like you have experienced freedom more than once in your life? Describe how you feel.

3) Would you consider asking for a prayer ministry session for yourself? Why or why not?

Chapter 28—Memory

1) If you have a memory that troubles you or makes you uncomfortable, can you see Jesus in the picture?

2) What is your reaction to the letter from Abba Father?

3) How do you address God/Jesus/Holy Spirit when you pray?

I hope you enjoyed this book and study guide! I invite you to contact me if I didn't address any issues you are interested in or if you have ideas of how I might share this book.

NOTES

Chapter 4—Black and White

1. *Merriam Webster*, s.v. "counselor (n.)," accessed December 14, 2021, https://www.merriam-webster.com/dictionary/counselor.

2. *Merriam Webster*, s.v. "therapist (n.), " accessed December 14, 2021, https://www.merriam-webster.com/dictionary/therapist.

3. *Merriam Webster*, s.v., "psychiatrist (n.)," https://www.merriam-webster.com/dictionary/psychiatrist.

Chapter 6—Flashbacks

"Mental Health: Overcoming the Stigma of Mental Illness," Mayo Clinic Staff, mayoclinic.org, accessed December 14, 2021, https://www.mayoclinic.org/diseases-conditions/mental-illness/in-depth/mental-health/art-20046477.

Chapter 8—Learning the Hard Way

1. Sarah Young, Jesus Calling—Enjoying Peace in His Presence (Nashville, TN: Thomas Nelson Publishing, 2004), 9.

Chapter 9—Was I Sexually Abused?

1. Jan Frank, *Door of Hope: Recognizing and Resolving the Pains of Your Past* (Nashville, TN: Thomas Nelson Publishing, 1987), 32.

2. David Peters, *Betrayal of Innocence What Everyone Should Know About Child Sexual Abuse* (Waco, TX: Word Books, 1986), 101.

Chapter 20—New Beginnings

1. *Merriam-Webster*, s.v. "out of sight, out of mind (idiom)," accessed December 14, 2021, https://www.merriam-webster.com/dictionary/out%20of%20sight%2C%20out%20of%20mind.

2. Poem: *"You Learn" and "After A While,"* is one half of a longer poem "Aprendiendo," which was written Spanish and which has been attributed to Jorge Luis Borges (August 24, 1899–14 June 1986), Argentinian poet, writer, and essayist. It is believed to have been written and published in the 1940s.

Chapter 21—Little Girl

1. Jeanie Connell, *I Can Grow Up-All I ever Needed to know About Being Grown-up I Learned from my Kids* (Laurens, South Carolina: Roots Outreach, 1996), 5-47.

2. Maxine Hancock, Karen Burton Mains, *Child Sexual Abuse: A Hope for Healing* (Harold Shaw Publisher, 1987), various.

3. "Autobiography in Five Short Chapters," a poem by Portia Nelson, 1977, *There's a Hole in My Sidewalk: The Romance of Self-Discovery* (New York: Atria Books, 2012, 35th anniversary edition), various.

Chapter 23—Illusion

1. Charles Dickens, *A Tale of Two Cities* (London: Chapman & Hall, 1859. Simon & Schuster May 1, 2004).

Chapter 25—One Flesh

1. Jeanie W. Connell, *God's Heartstrings—I Call His Name* (South Carolina: Booksurge, 2009).

2. Connell, *God's Heartstrings*…102–103.

Chapter 28—A Memory

1.Arlin Cuncic, "What Does It Mean to Be Triggered?" *verywellmind.com*, December 3, 2020, Medically reviewed by Carly Snyder, MD, https://www.verywellmind.com/what-does-it-mean-to-be-triggered-4175432.

RESOURCES

BOOKS:

Allender, Dan B. *The Wounded Heart: Hope for Adult Victims of Childhood Sexual Abuse.* NavPress, 1992.

Anderson, Neil T. *The Bondage Breaker: Overcoming Negative Thoughts, Irrational Feelings, Habitual Sins.* Eugene, Ore.: Harvest House, 1990.

Connell, Jeanie W. *God's Heartstrings—I Call His Name.* South Carolina; Book Surge, 2009. Amazon.com.

Connell, Jeanie. *I Can Grow Up—All I ever Needed to know About Being Grown-up I Learned from my Kids.* Laurens, South Carolina: Roots Outreach, 1996. jeanieconnell.org.:

Frank, Jan. *Door of Hope: Recognizing and Resolving the Pains of Your Past.* Nashville, Tennessee; Thomas Nelson, Inc, 1987.

Kraft, Charles H. *Christianity with Power.* Ann Arbor, Michigan; Servant Publications, 1989.

Kraft, Charles H. *Deep Wounds, Deep Healing.* Ann Arbor, Michigan: Servant Publications, 1993.

Kraft, Charles H. *Defeating Dark Angels.* Ann Arbor, Michigan: Servant Publications, 1992.

Peters, David B. *Betrayal of Innocence: What Everyone Should Know About Child Sexual Abuse.* Waco: Word Books, 1986.

Reese, Andy, and Jennifer Barnett. *Freedom Tools, For Overcoming Life's Tough Problems.* Ada, Michigan: Chosen Books, 2008. 2015.

Spell, Cynthia. *Deceived by Shame, Desired by God.* Carol Stream, Illinois: NavPress Publishing Group, December 15, 2001.

Thurman, Dr. Chris. *The Lies We Believe.* Nashville; Thomas Nelson, Inc, 1987.

CDs:

Connell, Jeanie W. *All I Have to Share,* including *Five Minutes for God.* Salisbury, North Carolina: Sandy Hoffman Music, 1986.

Connell, Jeanie. *I Call His Name.* Panama City, Florida: On-Da-Go Music, Producer Jamie McEachin, 2008.

Connell, Jeanie M. *Roots*. Hear! Hear! Studio, Ashville, North Carolina: Sandy Hoffman producer, 1992.

ABOUT THE AUTHOR

In addition to *Promise You Won't Remember—Becoming Whole When Pieces are Missing*, Jeanie Connell is also the author of *I Can Grow Up*, and *God's Heartstrings—I Call His Name*. She has recorded three CDs of her original music: *All I Have to Share, Roots, and I Call His Name*.

She is the CEO and founder of God's Heartstrings, sharing her childhood trauma through music and poetry. She is also certified with *American Association of Christian Counselors* (AACC) as a facilitator for "Caring for People God's Way."

Jeanie is part of a national Christian writing critique group, Word Weavers, International, and Franklin, Tennessee's Heartprint Writers' Group, which serves various genres.

Jeanie is also a worship leader and has a passion for intercessory prayer. She has led several women's retreats with that theme.

Jeanie and her husband Michael reside in Franklin, Tennessee. They have three married children and three grandchildren. You can reach out to her on her website: jeanieconnell.org.

Jeanie's passion is to share that we can *always* be assured of reaching Him, as we read in Jeremiah 33:3, "Call to Me and I will answer you and tell you great and unsearchable things that you do not know."

ACKNOWLEDGMENTS

Thanks to Michael, my husband of fifty years, for encouraging me to tell my story and allowing me to write parts of his own.

It is my belief that this book would never have come to print without the women across the United States who chose to pray for me when I sat in front of my computer.

My deepest thanks to Kathy Cain and Blayne Bosic in Riverside, California. To Heather Amberson in Gadsden, Alabama; Judi Weaber in Athens, Georgia; Linda Northouse in Freeport, Michigan; Mimi Mucher in DeBary, Florida; Rhonda Elliott in Ammon, Idaho; Vicki Bertrand in PCB, Florida; Mary J. Renneckar in Columbia, Missouri; Janice Conley in Lake Mary, Florida; and Nancy Moore in Casselberry, Florida. You girls have been my guardian angels, my encouragers, and my cheerleaders. May God reward you! Love to Kraft's and Burchfield's: Jesus with skin on, and Redemption City Church prayer group, Franklin, Tennessee. Special thanks to my prayer partner, Tonya Westbrook.

Thanks to Margaret May and William Warren for giving me birth, and Jesus for giving me Life.

Thanks to every doctor, psychiatrist, and therapist in these pages, some names are pseudonyms.

My thanks to Aqueduct Conference Center in Chapel Hill, North Carolina, and to Anne Hodges for inviting me there in 1993.

Thanks to Barbara Winter for opening her peaceful, spacious home in Florida to writers.

Thanks to Platinum Literary Services and Bethany Jett. I'm grateful to their developmental editor who read my manuscript and offered suggestions to make it better.

Thank You, Jesus, for Susan Neal's coaching through CIPA Director (Christian Indie Publishing Association), and thanks to 911EDIT for my line edit.

Thanks to Loral Pepoon with Selah Press Publishing for reaching out when I lost my editor. She is an answer to my prayers.

February 28, 2022, Jeanie Connell

Made in the USA
Coppell, TX
22 March 2022